READING COMPREHENSION IN THE ELEMENTARY SCHOOL

READING COMPREHENSION IN THE ELEMENTARY SCHOOL

A Teacher's Practical Guide

Robert M. Wilson
Linda B. Gambrell
University of Maryland

ALLYN AND BACON, INC.
Boston   London   Sydney   Toronto

Library of Congress Cataloging-in-Publication Data

Wilson, Robert Mills.
  Reading comprehension in the elementary school.

  Bibliography
  Includes index
  1. Reading (Elementary)—United States.   I. Gambrell,
Linda B.   II. Title.
LB1573.W548 1988   372.4   87-19468
ISBN 0-205-11161-0

Printed in the United States of America.

10 9 8 7 6 5 4 3 2 1   92 91 90 89 88 87

Contents

Preface

As we entered into the preparation of this book for elementary teachers, we felt a great sense of excitement. There are many interesting activities for teachers to consider as they plan their instruction in the area of reading comprehension, and we are excited about the opportunity to share our views on teaching reading comprehension with classroom teachers. We view reading comprehension instruction as the most important activity of elementary teachers. Their success in this endeavor will have an effect upon students for the remainder of their lives. It will determine, to a large extent, students' success in school, on the job, and in their personal lives.

We have worked to bring the most up-to-date information about reading comprehension to the classroom teacher. Our focus has been to provide teachers with many choices as they prepare for reading comprehension instruction. We know quite well that a given approach or strategy is not appropriate for all teachers or all students, so each teacher is an important decision maker with respect to reading comprehension instruction. In every chapter, teachers will have options from which they can make important instructional decisions. As they try new ideas, they must also evaluate those ideas as they observe their students responding to them. If something is not working very well, the teacher can make other choices in order to provide the best instruction for all students.

The suggestions in this book have been used successfully in elementary classrooms. We spend a lot of time working with elementary teachers, and we conduct the University of Maryland Summer Reading Clinic for students who are experiencing difficulties learning to read. In both of these situations we have received feedback on the value of recommended activities.

The specific strategies recommended in this book have also been the focus of current research. We, along with our students, have been conducting studies on strategies for enhancing reading comprehension for many years. Therefore, the strategies in this book have been field tested and are research based.

We hope you enjoy working with the ideas in this book, and we wish you and your students great success.

RMW

LBG

Getting Set for Reading Comprehension Instruction

1

Teachers should be viewed as decision makers in approaching instruction of any kind and especially instruction in the complicated area of reading comprehension. A teacher's decisions from among many available options can make great differences in students' understanding of text.

Teachers, of course, do not make decisions alone. Administrators, supervisors, students, and students' parents all affect their decision making. Their teacher's guides, fellow teachers, methods courses in college, and their view of the educational process are involved also. In this book we want to help teachers to assume as much decision-making responsibility as possible in assisting students to understand text. A school system might direct teachers to use a particular text or method; the individual teacher is the one who must decide just how to use that text or method.

While teachers might be responsive to parental concern about given procedures, each particular teacher remains accountable for the education of all the students in his or her class. If students seem unresponsive to a given teaching strategy or instructional material, the teacher must become a decision maker. Regardless of the constraints that teachers might feel, they still have many important decisions to make.

We intend this book to clarify the options available to teachers and to help them to understand the consequences of their decisions for various types of students.

At the start of this text, we want to make one thing very clear: We believe that teachers are important decision makers; they could not teach without being so, whether right or wrong.

Teachers make decisions at different times during the school year, week, or day. While it is a bit difficult to delineate all of the decisions that teachers need to make, we will categorize them as follows:

- decisions about classroom atmosphere
- decisions about planning
- decisions about instruction
- decisions about follow-up
- decisions about homework

DECISIONS ABOUT CLASSROOM ATMOSPHERE

There are some decisions that teachers can make to enhance reading comprehension through the adjustment of the classroom atmosphere. They can have displays of interesting books and magazines. They can have interesting resource materials in the classroom to help children acquire new knowledge. They can set up a quiet area for pleasure reading and learning centers where students can study interesting topics independently. Many teachers keep a book that they are reading on their desk. This tends to model reading as an enjoyable activity. Many teachers also make sure that all students have a book in their desk for recreational reading. They make certain that students understand that recreational reading is an appropriate free-time activity. Bulletin boards can be used to display exciting books and authors. Students' writing about exciting things they have read can be displayed for others to read. These types of adjustments are easily done and contribute to making the classroom an environment in which reading is viewed as a desirable activity.

Many aspects of classroom atmosphere are common to all areas of instruction. They involve such factors as room cleanliness and attractiveness. They include room temperature, suitable seating for students, proper lighting, and access to out-of-classroom activities, such as libraries and resource teachers' rooms. These aspects of classroom atmosphere management can have an effect on whether or not students even want to come to school at all. While they are not limited to the area of reading comprehension, they would be considered first by most teachers regardless of the area of instruction. For example, if students were complaining about classroom noise or temperature, most teachers would attempt to make some adjustments.

DECISIONS ABOUT PLANNING

Prior to actual instruction teachers need to make many decisions involving their plans for instruction. These decisions involve the areas of

- student preassessment
- selection of materials for instruction
- student grouping
- lesson format
- time allocation

Student preassessment. Teachers usually have a lot of information about their students' abilities and knowledge about given topics. Sometimes this information is collected informally and over an extended period of time. When starting new units or when introducing new concepts, a more careful preassessment is often needed. For example, if a new unit is being introduced on the topic of "Life in the Old West," it would be useful to ask some questions directed at finding out just what the students already know about this topic. Or if an instruction is to focus on critical reading, it would be useful to know something about the critical reading abilities the students have already mastered. In both cases, some planned assessment of the students' knowledge or ability in these areas would be of great help.

If teachers fail to consider this step in their planning they might be guilty of assumptive teaching (Herber, 1978). Herber explained assumptive teaching as follows: For various reasons, teachers sometimes assume that their students have knowledge or skills. They might assume that these areas have been taught before or that the areas are common knowledge for their students. Assumptive teaching is a real trap for the students as well as for the teacher; the teacher may proceed with instruction that is over the heads of the students. The teacher *assumes* that the instruction is appropriate, but it might not be. When assessed, the students do poorly. The teacher again *assumes* that the fault lies within the students; however, in fact, it was a teacher mistake. We have all been in classes in which we were exposed to assumptive teaching. Remember the college history professor who assumed that you knew the causes of the War of 1812 and then went on enthusiastically to discuss the outcomes of that war? It made you feel confused and stupid, right? It takes only one such experience to make one realize the hazards of assumptive teaching. On the other hand, if the teacher has already made an assessment about the students' skills or knowledge, a formal preassessment is not necessary.

Teachers must be aware that assumptive teaching can make the difference between a student's learning or not learning: between his or her being comfortable or frustrated in the learning situation.

Selection of materials for instruction. From the many materials available for instruction teachers need to make decisions in the best interest of their students. Which materials are best suited to the comprehension skills to be taught? Which will best hold the students' attention? Do different materials need to be selected for various groups of students? Are the needed materials available to the class, or must they be obtained from sources outside the classroom? Will the text be narrative or expository? How much text will be appropriate for the various student groups to comprehend without difficulty? These types of decisions about materials need to be made prior to instruction and can have an enormous impact upon the effectiveness of that instruction.

Student grouping. Deciding which students can be grouped best for instruction is also very important. Students might be grouped together for reading instruction because of their interest in the topic to be read or because of their level or skill development in a given area. At times students might be grouped together so that they can

Dr. David Williams

help each other. This type of grouping might have very skilled readers working with those who are less skilled.

Many teachers use a variety of group strategies and view any group as a temporary arrangement for instruction. When using groups in this manner, the teacher makes daily decisions about grouping. Each decision can have an effect on student learning and on the student's concept of self as a reader.

Lesson format. An important part of lesson planning has to do with lesson format. What are the lesson objectives? What skills need to be included in the lesson? Are these skills to be reviewed, or will this be initial instruction? What steps are needed to prepare the students to gain the most from a given lesson? Exactly what type of teacher–student interaction will best suit the objectives of this lesson? Will the lesson be largely teacher-directed or will students be directing their own learning? What type of feedback will be provided for the students? In what part of the classroom will students be working? Will they need to move from one part of the classroom to another? How will this movement be managed to cause as little confusion as possible? Lesson format decisions have a direct bearing on the type of learning that can be expected and on how learning can be managed effectively.

Time allocation. When considering the above, decisions about the factor of timing in reading comprehension lessons are important. Timing involves some of the following concerns: How much time will be spent on direct instruction? How much time will be spent on follow-up activities? If the lesson starts to go stale, what alternatives can put some excitement back into the lesson? What activities can be planned for those students who finish their work early? What should be planned for students who do not have enough time to finish their work?

DECISIONS ABOUT INSTRUCTION

Once the classroom atmosphere has been established and careful consideration has been given to planning, the teacher can concentrate on the various aspects of instruction. While instruction can be carefully planned, there are many decisions to be made during the instructional time. For various reasons, students do not always respond to the plans in the manner that the teacher anticipates. For example, some students might not be able to respond to the instruction because they have not mastered the prerequisite skills. The teacher might need to represent ideas in a manner different from the plans. More or less time might be needed for various aspects of the lesson. Materials might need to be adjusted. The amount of teacher-directed activities might need to be increased or decreased. There are times when instruction might need to be adjusted because of other activities that are occurring in that area of the classroom. Fire drills, announcements from the office, and special needs of some students are a few more examples of activities that can cause a need for a change of plans during instruction. At times incorrect assessments of student abilities and interests will call for instructional adjustments.

Teachers, therefore, need to be flexible and willing to change their plans in the interest of their students' learning. Some students might need more help than anticipated with their follow-up work. This might call for an adjustment concerning the instructional time allocated to other students. Most teachers have experienced a situation in which almost everything went wrong and a given lesson simply had to be scrapped. While careful planning can make this a very unusual occasion, it will happen!

Teacher response to students' work is a vital aspect of instruction. Whether the students' work is wholly accurate, partially accurate, or very inaccurate, the teacher's responses during instruction can have a strong effect on students' future efforts.

Since much of reading comprehension is a matter of personal interpretation, care must be taken not to be overly critical or negative about students' efforts. Rather, teachers will want to plan their instruction so that students can gain as much understanding as possible from text. Working with partially accurate and inaccurate student responses to assist students in gaining a clearer understanding of a text is key to effective instruction in reading comprehension.

Teachers also need to decide on instructional strategies for the various groups of students with whom they will be working. A given strategy that might work well with one group might not work well with another. Teachers will need to be aware of instructional strategies and their advantages and limitations. More information about strategies will be provided in upcoming chapters.

DECISIONS ABOUT
FOLLOW-UP

After direct instruction from the teacher, students are usually expected to complete some work to reinforce what they have just learned. Follow-up activities are usually not closely monitored by the teacher, who is likely to be working with another group of students in direct instruction. This means that follow-up activities should be of such a nature that students can complete them independently or at least with a minimum of teacher supervision. Normally follow-up activities are directly related to the preceding direct instructional activities. This provides the greatest assurance that the students can complete the work successfully.

Students should be aware of the purposes of follow-up activities so that they know how the activities can be of benefit to them. They should also understand when they have fulfilled the purposes of the activities so that they will know when they are finished. They should have a clear understanding of appropriate activities for them to become engaged in when they have completed the assigned follow-up activities. This understanding lessens the possibility of student activities that might be distracting to those who are still trying to complete their follow-up activities.

DECISIONS ABOUT
HOMEWORK

Most teachers expect students to make some preparation at home for school. This is especially true for reading comprehension. Homework assignments are similar to follow-up activities in school. That is, they should be related to recent direct instruction, and they should be activities that the students can complete independently. There are times, however, when homework assignments relate to future in-school instruction. For example, students might be asked to bring examples of figurative language from the sports page of the daily newspaper to be used in an upcoming lesson on figurative language. In-school practice with this type of activity helps to assure that the activity can be completed independently. For example, a teacher might model the importance for tomorrow's lesson by bringing his or her old newspapers by and guide students to identify figurative language from the sports pages.

At times a teacher might want parents to help their children with homework. Most parents are eager to do so. When making this type of homework assignment, the teacher should be sure that there is someone at home who is available to help and can do so in a constructive manner. A note to parents about what is expected often helps.

The teacher should have established policies for dealing with students who do not complete their homework assignments. There is, of course, a range of excuses deserving consideration. However, students need to be aware that homework assignments can play an important part in the next day's learning process and that coming to school unprepared diminishes the likelihood of getting the most from in-school instruction.

CHAPTER SUMMARY

This first chapter provides an overview of some of the many decisions that teachers need to make for effective instruction in general and for reading comprehension instruction in particular.

The remainder of this book will deal with the specifics of reading comprehension instruction in the elementary classroom. The benefits and problems associated with teacher decisions about reading comprehension instruction will be presented.

REFERENCE

Herber, H. L. (1978). *Teaching Reading in the Content Areas*, 2nd ed., Englewood Cliffs, N. J.: Prentice-Hall.

Reading Comprehension Instruction

2

Reading comprehension instruction has been the topic of much debate in recent years. Observations of classroom reading instruction have consistently revealed that there is an emphasis on subskill activities and teacher-posed questions, and there is little, if any, attention given to reading comprehension instruction. For example, students are frequently asked to respond to a variety of questions about what they have read, but they are rarely given instruction on how to go about answering these questions. Indeed, Durkin (1978–79) found that teachers rarely provided explicit instruction on the use of comprehension strategies. In an analysis of basal readers and teachers' manuals Durkin (1981) found that manuals directed teachers to engage in question-and-answer sessions about the content of the stories, but they offered little instruction about strategies to improve comprehension.

Our contention is that students should develop a repertoire of reading comprehension strategies. Students should be able to identify the purpose for reading and then be able to draw from their repertoire an appropriate strategy for enhancing their comprehension of the text. The primary goals of this chapter are to present some basic definitions of reading, reading comprehension, and reading comprehension instruction and to present a basic model for reading comprehension instruction.

WHAT IS READING?

There is no simple answer to this seemingly simple question. Educators and psychologists have generated literally hundreds of definitions of the very complex reading process. In general, most agree that reading is a process involving both decoding and comprehension. Decoding refers to the breaking of the visual code of symbols (letters) into sounds, while comprehension refers to the understanding of the message. Any definition of reading, however, should recognize the importance of the ultimate goal of the reading process: comprehension. Whether one is reading a story, a definition of a word in a dictionary, the sports page, directions for putting together a model airplane, a recipe, an encyclopedia, or the directions for cooking frozen green beans, the primary objective of the reader is to make sense of the message.

WHAT IS READING COMPREHENSION?

Any definition of reading comprehension must take into account the interaction between the reader and the text. Each reader brings to the reading process a unique combination of interests, motivation, attitudes, skills, and background of experiences. Each text also has unique characteristics that can influence comprehension. The readability of the text, concept density, passage coherence, and passage organization are just a few text characteristics that have been shown to influence reading comprehension. Thus, reading comprehension can be defined as the process of using one's own prior experiences and text cues to infer the author's intended meaning (Irwin, 1986; Johnston, 1981).

WHAT IS READING COMPREHENSION INSTRUCTION?

Durkin's (1978–79) research, which involved classroom observations of reading instruction, revealed that little reading comprehension instruction took place. Instead, she found that teachers frequently "mentioned" comprehension but rarely provided explicit instruction. Durkin characterized teachers as being assignment givers, assignment checkers, and interrogators. Her research has drawn attention to the gap that has existed in the knowledge base about the reading process and reading comprehension instruction. Recent research and classroom practice have focused upon how teachers might provide more effective reading comprehension instruction in American schools (Duffy, Roehler, & Mason, 1984; Anderson, Hiebert, Scott, & Wilkinson, 1985).

The goal of reading comprehension instruction is to teach students to identify and employ appropriate strategies to facilitate and enhance comprehension of text. The following tenets are central to basic notions about reading comprehension instruction:

1. Comprehension monitoring facilitates the intentional use of appropriate reading comprehension strategies.
2. Reading comprehension strategies can be explicitly taught to students.
3. Self-directed use of reading comprehension strategies is developed through instruction that gradually shifts the learning responsibility from the teacher to the student.

Comprehension monitoring facilitates the intentional use of appropriate reading comprehension strategies. Comprehension monitoring is the deliberate, conscious control of one's own level of reading comprehension (Brown, 1980). Comprehension monitoring occurs when readers begin to scrutinize their comprehension processes and actively evaluate and regulate comprehension processes. In short, comprehension monitoring occurs when readers think about their own comprehension and take remedial action to rectify comprehension failure (Devine, 1986; Wagoner, 1983). There is substantial research that suggests that mature and better readers are aware of their level of comprehension, while younger and poorer readers often are unaware that comprehension failure has occurred (Brown, 1980; Wagoner, 1983). Before a reader can independently employ specific strategies to enhance comprehension, there must be an awareness on the reader's part that comprehension is less than adequate. Research evidence suggests that an important component of comprehension instruction involves developing comprehension-monitoring abilities (Baker & Brown, 1984).

Students need to develop an awareness of and sensitivity to their own level of comprehension processing. They should also be aware of the kinds of difficulties that might occur during the reading process and what to do when these difficulties occur. Collins and Smith (1980) have identified four major categories of comprehension failure and presented reasons as to why failure might occur:

1. *Failure to understand a word* might occur because of an encounter with a word that
   - is an unknown word
   - is a known word that doesn't make sense in the context
2. *Failure to understand a sentence* might occur because
   - you can find no interpretation
   - you can find only a vague, abstract interpretation
   - you can find several possible interpretations (ambiguous sentence)
   - your interpretation conflicts with prior knowledge
3. *Failure to understand how one sentence relates to another* might occur because
   - your interpretation of one sentence conflicts with another
   - you can find no connection between the sentences
   - you can find several possible connections between the sentences
4. *Failure to understand how the whole text fits together* might occur because
   - you can find no point to the whole or part of the text

- you do not understand why certain episodes or sections occurred
- you do not understand the motivations of certain characters

According to Irwin (1986) the most important "process used by readers to get meaning is monitoring their own comprehension for success or failure" (p. 86). In order to become strategic in their reading behaviors, students should be aware of the occurrence of comprehension failure; they should know how comprehension failures can occur, and they should have a repertoire of strategies for remedying the situation.

Collins and Smith (1980) have suggested a series of six steps for resolving comprehension failure:

1. *Ignore the difficulty and read on.* The information may be relatively unimportant.
2. *Suspend judgment.* The difficulty may be cleared up later.
3. *Form a tentative hypothesis.* The hypothesis can be tested as reading continues.
4. *Reread the sentence(s).* This may clear up the difficulty or pinpoint the difficulty.
5. *Reread the previous context.* This may clear up the difficulty or pinpoint the contradiction.
6. *Go to an expert source.* This may be necessary when steps 1 to 5 have not resulted in resolving the comprehension failure and the text still does not make sense.

Skilled readers are strategic. They monitor progress in understanding and they have strategies available for resolving problems that prevent understanding. Since younger and less skilled readers do not spontaneously monitor their comprehension processing, they need to be placed in instructional settings where they can learn to be successful at comprehension monitoring (Mason, Roehler, & Duffy, 1984).

Reading comprehension strategies can be explicitly taught to students. According to Paris (1986) a strategy is more than a successful action. For example, a person could make a hole-in-one while playing golf simply by accident. Similarly, students sometimes correctly answer questions about what they have read for reasons other than the deployment of efficient reading comprehension strategies. Students might successfully answer teacher questions about what they have read by guessing. Students can also be successful by explicitly following the directions of the teacher. The teacher might say, for example, "Find the paragraph that describes the appearance of the main character." The successful completion of these reading tasks, however, does not necessarily reflect specific strategy deployment on the part of the reader. Without knowledge about specific strategies for enhancing reading comprehension, students may not know how to transfer successful actions to other reading tasks.

A reading comprehension strategy is a specific plan of action implemented by the reader toward the goal of obtaining meaning from the text. Reading comprehension instruction provides information directly to students about various strategies that can facilitate and enhance reading comprehension. Reading comprehension strategies can be explicitly taught to students using elements of *informed teaching* (Paris, 1986). Informed teaching simply means that the teacher tells students *what* reading comprehension strategy will be taught, *how* it operates, *when* it is most appropriately used, and *why* it should be used (Paris, 1986). Reading comprehension instruction is also characterized by "extensive discussion and teacher–student interaction so that students can increase their understanding about reading as well as their skills and motivation" (Paris, 1986, p. 117).

Self-directed use of reading comprehension strategies is developed through instruction that gradually shifts the learning responsibility from the teacher to the student. Strategic readers combine knowledge about the reading task with motivation to act accordingly. However, self-directed use of reading comprehension strategies is unlikely to occur, according to Brown (1980), if students are uninformed about reading comprehension strategies and their utility or if they are not motivated to use the strategies. If we expect students to be self-directed in their use of reading comprehension strategies in both an appropriate and spontaneous manner, it is essential that students perceive that the strategies are both sensible and useful courses of action (Paris, 1986).

Self-directed use of reading comprehension strategies is facilitated by instruction that is characterized by guided practice, feedback, faded support, and generalization to other reading situations (Pearson & Gallagher, 1983). The ultimate goal of reading comprehension instruction is that the strategies will be self-controlled by the reader; that is, the reader will have *ownership* of the strategies and will be able to use the strategies appropriately as personal resources for enhancing comprehension of text.

The role of the teacher is indeed critical within the framework of reading comprehension instruction, for it is the teacher who guides the student toward the independent use of reading comprehension strategies. How does the teacher teach reading comprehension instead of just mentioning or measuring it? In this chapter we are going to suggest the Guided Strategy Instruction procedure for reading comprehension instruction.

GUIDED STRATEGY INSTRUCTION

The Guided Strategy Instruction procedure involves four basic steps for teaching students *what* reading comprehension strategies are available, *why* students should use them, *how* they operate, and *when* they should most appropriately be used. The four basic steps in Guided Strategy Instruction are listed below, along with the continuum of responsibility, from teacher-directed (explanation) to student-directed (independent application).

Guided Strategy Instruction

Instructional Step	*Responsibility*
1. Explanation	Teacher
2. Demonstration	Teacher
3. Guided Practice	Teacher/Student
4. Independent Application	Student

Guided Strategy Instruction emphasizes the importance of (1) providing students with a rationale for using reading comprehension strategies (explanation), (2) modeling how a strategy is implemented (demonstration), (3) providing teacher-guided practice that empha- sizes feedback and faded teacher support (guided practice), and (4) shifting responsibility to use reading strategies from the teacher to the student so that learning is self-directed (independent application).

1. Explanation. In this initial step of Guided Strategy Instruction the teacher answers two important questions related to the compre- hension strategy to be taught: *What* strategy is to be taught, and *why* should students use the strategy? From the information available from observational studies of classroom practice it appears that one of the most common features of instruction is "repeated exposure." Students are given repeated practice in doing an activity with little, if any, attention to *why* or *how* to be successful at implementing the strategy or technique (Durkin, 1978–79; Duffy & Roehler, 1982). In Guided Strategy Instruction the teacher introduces the specific strategy and provides a rationale for using the strategy. Providing a rationale for employing a specific comprehension strategy provides motivation for strategy implementation.

Paris (1986) has suggested that metaphors may serve an important function in explaining reading strategies and making them more "con- crete" for the learner. His research indicated that the use of metaphors seems to make comprehension strategies sensible to students. Some of the metaphors used to explain reading comprehension behaviors included the following:

- Summarizing: "Round Up Your Ideas"
- Reading for Purposes: "Be a Reading Detective"
- Identifying the Main Idea: "Track Down the Main Idea"

Students will be motivated to learn and internalize reading com- prehension strategies if they perceive them as useful, appropriate, and sensible. Providing a simple, concrete rationale for learning a specific comprehension strategy is an important first step.

2. Demonstration. In the second step of Guided Strategy Instruc- tion the teacher models how the procedure would be used during the reading process. One way of describing and demonstrating how to implement strategies would be for the teacher to use a think-aloud procedure. Using the think-aloud procedure the teacher verbalizes thinking processes and describes *how* and *when* the specific comprehension strategy is used during text processing (Davey & Porter, 1982). Discrimination activities can also play an important role in demonstrating how to use reading comprehension strategies. For example, if summarizing is a strategy that is being introduced, the teacher might present three summaries of a passage and then indicate why one is *not* a good example of a summary while another meets the criteria for a good summary. The discrimination activity provides a meaningful opportunity for the teacher to focus on the characteristics of a good summary and to model how a person would read a passage and then construct an appropriate summary. The demonstration step is probably the most critical step in the basic teaching model. In this step the teacher goes beyond *telling* the students to use a strategy and provides a model for *how* to implement the strategy.

3. Guided practice. In the third step the teacher guides students through the use of the strategy. This step provides students with guided practice in using the strategy. We suggest that teachers select brief passages or introductory paragraphs of text to use with students during initial teacher-guided practice sessions and then move to lengthier texts.

In the guided practice step it is important for the teacher to remember that when students experience uncertainty or confusion the teacher should provide guidance. Some students will need only brief experience with teacher-guided practice before becoming independent in using the strategy. Some students, however, will need repeated experiences with teacher-guided practice before they are able to employ a reading comprehension strategy independently.

Guided practice sessions should culminate in a discussion about the specific reading comprehension strategy that has been practiced. The students discuss the strategy: How did it work? Did it require a lot of effort? Was it useful? Students need the opportunity to discuss and share their reactions to strategy employment. Opportunities to describe, question, and defend strategy usage emphasize the personal aspects of reading strategies and the idea that there is not always a "best" strategy. There is substantial research that suggests that interactive discussions facilitate learning (Paris, 1986). Discussions about strategy usage help to "make thinking public" so that students can learn from one another. The interactive learning that occurs during discussions is an important step in shifting the responsibility for applying and using strategies from the teacher to the student.

4. Independent application. In the final step of Guided Strategy Instruction explicit teacher support fades and students assume responsibility for applying the strategies independently. When students are comfortable with a particular strategy the teacher provides appropriate instructional text and the students are instructed to use the strategy independently. The teacher plays a crucial role in this step that is often overlooked. Not only must the teacher provide appropriate instructional materials, but the teacher must also provide motivation for the students to use the strategy in their independent reading and studying. One way that teachers can encourage self-directed usage is to remind and encourage students to employ specific strategies during independent reading. Another way to encourage self-directed strategy usage is through providing "bridging lessons" periodically (Paris, 1986). In a bridging lesson the teacher uses selections from science, social studies, and other content areas to provide opportunities for independent strategy usage. In this way students learn that the strategies can be applied *beyond* the reading comprehension lesson.

GUIDED STRATEGY
INSTRUCTION—AN EXAMPLE

Here is an example of how a teacher might use Guided Strategy Instruction to teach students to use mental imagery as a comprehension strategy.

Explanation

> *Teacher*: Readers sometimes make pictures in their minds about what they are reading. Making pictures in your mind is one strategy you can use to understand and remember what you are reading. Today we will all try to make pictures in our mind about what we read.

In this step the teacher has introduced the specific comprehension strategy and has provided a rationale for *why* it is a good strategy to use when learning from text.

Demonstration

> *Teacher*: I have a short story, *The Desert Man*, which I am going to read aloud to you. I am going to try to make pictures in my head about what I read. I will describe how I use mental imagery to help me understand and remember what I read.

The teacher has selected the following text to use for demonstrating mental imagery as a comprehension strategy:

THE DESERT MAN

The old man was hot and tired. His long white robe billowed in the dry desert wind. He wiped his brow as he started to trudge up yet another of the endless dunes of the desert. He saw only a sea of sand surrounding him. The sun beat down on him mercilessly. He would not give up. He knew the camp was near.

At this point in the demonstration the teacher proceeds to read aloud the text and to think aloud about the use of mental imagery. In the following example the text of *The Desert Man* appears in capital letters and the teacher's think-aloud procedure appears in lower case.

> *Teacher*: The title of the story is *The Desert Man* . . . I have a pretty good picture in my mind of what the desert looks like. Miles and miles of sand, blazing hot, very little vegetation. "THE OLD MAN WAS HOT AND TIRED. HIS LONG WHITE ROBE BILLOWED IN THE DRY DESERT WIND." My picture in my head is of a very old man. He is dressed in a long white robe. The material must be light enough to be blown in the wind. I can see the wind blowing his robe. "HE WIPED HIS BROW AS HE STARTED TO TRUDGE UP YET ANOTHER OF THE ENDLESS DUNES OF THE DESERT. HE SAW ONLY A SEA OF SAND SURROUNDING HIM" . . . I can see in my own mind what the old man sees: miles and miles of desert . . . Perhaps he is wiping his brow because he is hot and weary. "THE SUN BEAT DOWN ON HIM MERCILESSLY. HE WOULD NOT GIVE UP. HE KNEW THE CAMP WAS NEAR" . . . The look on the old man's face is very

clear to me now. He has a look of determination on his face. He is very determined to locate the camp. The pictures I made in my mind about this passage will help me understand and remember what I have read. This is a comprehension strategy *you* can use when you read.

In this step the teacher has modeled the mental imagery strategy using a think-aloud procedure. At the conclusion of the demonstration the teacher has again emphasized the rationale for using mental imagery as a comprehension strategy.

Guided Practice

Teacher: I have a short passage I would like you to read silently. The title of the story is *The Attic Room*. Can you picture in your mind what an attic room might look like? This story begins in an attic room. Try to make pictures in your mind to help you understand and remember what happens in this story.

THE ATTIC ROOM

It was early morning and Beth was looking out the window in her little attic room, waiting for the clock on the church steeple to strike 7 o'clock. It was already warm and her window was open wide. There was only a small breeze. It was going to be a very warm summer day. From her window Beth had the best view of the church steeple in the whole town. That was why this was her favorite place.

Teacher: Tell me about the pictures you made in your mind about Beth and the attic room. Tell me about your pictures of what the church looks like.

In this step the teacher has provided teacher-guided practice. An appropriate text for the specific strategy (mental imagery) has been selected. The teacher has introduced the procedure and has provided an opportunity for students to employ the strategy. The culmination of the guided practice step is to promote discussion of strategy usage.

Some examples of questions that teachers might use to stimulate discussion of strategy usage are given below.

> *Teacher*: Who can describe how the mental imagery strategy works for them? Why do you think it works for you? What makes it a good comprehension strategy? When would this strategy be most useful? Was there a particular part of the text where you thought the strategy was most effective?

Independent Application

> *Teacher*: Today, we are going to read a story called *McCreedy Tells a Lie*. We have been using mental imagery to help understand and remember what we read. I would like for you to make pictures in your mind about the things you read in this story.

Students silently read the story and employ the mental imagery strategy.)

> *Teacher*: Tell me about the pictures you get of the kind of life McCreedy lived out in the wilderness. Tell me about the pictures you get about the kind of life his friend lived in Hawaii.

At the conclusion of the discussion of the story where students have been given an opportunity to apply independently the mental imagery strategy, the teacher should encourage independent application of the strategy to other stories and other content areas.

> *Teacher*: Now you have used mental imagery as a comprehension strategy to help you understand and remember what you read. Tonight, when you read your history assignment I would like for you to use the mental imagery strategy to help you understand and remember the important ideas about the Battle of Bull Run.

In this step the teacher has provided opportunities for the independent application of the mental imagery strategy. Independent application of the strategy has also been extended to other stories or other content area assignments.

Using the Guided Strategy Instruction procedure presented here should help students successfully develop a repertoire of comprehension strategies. The four steps of the Guided Strategy Instruction procedure provide a continuum toward developing independent student use of comprehension strategies. Usually, instruction would include all four steps when a specific comprehension strategy is initially introduced. Some steps in the basic teaching model may need to be repeated before proceeding to the next step with some students. The teacher may decide that with some students it is helpful to provide instruction using the *explanation* and *demonstration* steps several times before proceeding with *guided practice*. Some students may only need to go through the processes of *explanation* and *demonstration* once. Guided practice is a crucial step where the teacher must assess the proficiency of the students in using the strategy. Several teacher-guided sessions may be necessary for some students with some strategies. Equally important, with respect to independent application, is the notion that students should be aware of their own repertoire of comprehension strategies. Teachers can facilitate strategy awareness by providing opportunities for students to select and use specific comprehension strategies independently.

After students have developed independence in using several comprehension strategies, the teacher can present instructional material and have students select a comprehension strategy. Discussion can then focus on why particular strategies were chosen and the importance of matching strategy employment with text characteristics.

UNDERSTANDING CONTENT AND STRATEGY—SOME DISTINCTIONS

The emphasis in this chapter has been on the importance of developing student ownership of reading comprehension strategies, however, both *instruction for comprehending text* and *instruction in strategies for comprehending text* are important aspects of reading comprehension instruction (Mason, Roehler, & Duffy, 1984). In instruction for comprehending text the goal of the teacher is to facilitate and guide the students in understanding the text content. Understanding the *content* is the primary goal. The Directed Reading Activity and other teaching procedures detailed in Chapter 5 are examples of instruction that is directed toward understanding text. On the other hand, the goal of instruction in strategies for comprehending text, as exemplified by the Guided Strategy Instruction procedure detailed in this chapter, is to have students *understand the strategy* and use it for understanding the content of the text.

There is some debate about whether reading comprehension strategies should be directly taught or whether strategies for comprehending text develop naturally from instruction in comprehending text (Duffy, Roehler, & Mason, 1984). Classroom observational research indicates that the reading lessons in elementary classes are primarily, if not exclusively, based on instruction for comprehending text (Durkin, 1978–79). Recent research suggests that instruction in *strategies* for comprehending text results in improved reading comprehension performance (Paris, 1986). It seems reasonable that both approaches are important and fruitful ways of providing reading comprehension instruction.

THE ROLE OF COMPREHENSION INSTRUCTION

It is important to keep in mind that reading comprehension instruction should take place across the curriculum. For most elementary students reading comprehension instruction will probably take place during teacher-directed reading instruction. The Guided Strategy Instruction procedure can be used during teacher-directed reading instruction to teach students specific comprehension strategies; however, it is equally important that reading comprehension instruction take place in the content areas. It is also important that students realize that some strategies may be more appropriate to use to enhance their reading for personal pleasure (e.g., mental imagery) and that some strategies may be more appropriate for use with specific expository materials in areas such as science and social studies (e.g., outlining).

Teacher-directed reading instruction. We suggest that the teacher-directed reading instructional period is the appropriate time to introduce and teach strategies for comprehension of text. Teachers can identify and teach an appropriate strategy so that students are comfortable and independent in their use of the strategy before introducing a second strategy. As teachers plan out their teaching of reading comprehension strategies, we suggest that they start with strategies that will be easy for their students to learn and use independently. Not all of the strategies presented in this text will be appropriate for all students. The teacher will need to consider the characteristics of the students and select appropriate strategies accordingly. One important goal should be that students have command of several reading comprehension strategies they can use to help them understand and remember text information. Each student should be aware of strategies to use for enhancing text processing (see Chapter 5) and strategies to use for reorganizing text information (see Chapter 6).

Content area reading. Our contention is that the Guided Strategy Instruction procedure presented in this chapter should also be used in the content areas to specifically teach the application of reading comprehension strategies to content area textbooks. The term *content area* is used here to describe content subjects, such as science, history, and social studies, as they are taught in the elementary, middle, and secondary schools. Each of the strategies presented in Chapters 5 and 6 can be directly applied or adapted for use in any of the content areas.

Recreational reading. The role of reading comprehension strategy use in recreational reading has typically not been dealt with in the reading literature. There is evidence that good readers employ specific strategies for enhancing their pleasure and understanding of reading done for personal pleasure (Olshavsky, 1976–77). Therefore, we suggest that teachers guide students in developing an awareness of the importance of certain process strategies, such as predicting and mental imagery in recreational reading as well as in content area reading.

CHAPTER SUMMARY

In this chapter some basic definitions of *reading, reading comprehension,* and *reading comprehension instruction* were presented. The

Guided Strategy Instruction procedure was presented as a model for teaching specific reading comprehension strategies. The four steps of the Guided Strategy Instruction procedure are (1) explanation, (2) demonstration, (3) guided practice, and (4) independent application. The distinction between teaching comprehension of text and teaching *strategies* for comprehending text was made. While it is probably the most appropriate to introduce and teach reading comprehension during teacher-directed reading instruction, emphasizing strategies for comprehending text in content areas and in recreational reading is important.

REFERENCES

Anderson, R. C., Hiebert, E. F., Scott, J. A., & Wilkinson, I.A.G. (1985). *Becoming a nation of readers.* Washington, D.C.: The National Institute of Education.

Baker, L., & Brown, A. L. (1984). Metacognitive skills and reading. In P. D. Pearson (Ed.) *Handbook of reading research* (pp. 353–394). New York: Longman.

Brown, A. (1980). Metacognitive development and reading. In R. J. Spiro, B. Bruce, & W. F. Brewer (Eds.), *Theoretical issues in reading comprehension* (pp. 453–481). Hillsdale, N. J.: Erlbaum.

Collins, A. & Smith, E. E. (1980). *Teaching the process of reading comprehension.* (Technical Report No. 182). Urbana-Champaign: Center for the Study of Reading, University of Illinois.

Davey, B., & Porter, S. M. (1982). Comprehension-rating: A procedure to assist poor comprehenders. *Journal of Reading. 26,* 197–202.

Devine, T. G. (1986). *Teaching reading comprehension: From theory to practice.* Newton, Mass.: Allyn and Bacon.

Duffy, G., & Roehler, L. (1982). The illusion of instruction. *Reading Research Quarterly, 17,* 438–445.

Duffy, G. G., Roehler, L. R., & Mason, J. (1984). The reality and potential of comprehension instruction. In G. G. Duffy, L. R. Roehler, & J. Mason (Eds.), *Comprehension instruction: Perspectives and suggestions* (pp. 3–9). New York: Longman.

Durkin, D. (1978–79). What classroom observations reveal about reading comprehension instruction. *Reading Research Quarterly. 14,* 481–533.

Durkin, D. (1981). Reading comprehension instruction in five basal reading series. *Reading Research Quarterly, 16,* 525–544.

Irwin, J. W. (1986). *Teaching reading comprehension processes.* Englewood Cliffs, N.J.: Prentice-Hall.

Johnston, P. (1981). *Implications of basic research for the assessment of reading comprehension* (Technical Report no. 206). Urbana-Champaign: Center for the Study of Reading, University of Illinois.

Mason, J., Roehler, L. R., & Duffy, G. G. (1984). A practitioner's model of comprehension instruction. In G. G. Duffy, L. R. Roehler, & J. Mason (Eds.), *Compre-*

hension instruction: Perspectives and suggestions (pp. 299–314). New York: Longman.

Olshavsky, J. E. (1976–77). Reading as problem solving: An investigation of strategies. *Reading Research Quarterly. 12*, 654–674.

Paris, S. G. (1986). Teaching children to guide their reading and learning. In T. E. Raphael & R. Reynolds (Eds.), *Contexts of literacy* (pp. 115–130). New York: Longman.

Pearson, P. D., & Gallagher, M. C. (1983). The instruction of reading comprehension. *Contemporary Educational Psychology, 8*, 317–344.

Wagoner, S. (1983). Comprehension monitoring: What it is and what we know about it. *Reading Research Quarterly, 18*, 328–346.

Strategies for Enhancing Text Processing

3

This chapter will focus on comprehension strategies that students can employ *during the process* of reading text. Students can employ these specific strategies in order to facilitate the comprehension process in general or when they realize that comprehension failure has occurred and additional effort must be expended in order to gain meaning from the text. There is ample evidence that good readers *spontaneously* employ specific strategies that facilitate the comprehension of text (Olshavsky, 1976–77). Some readers, however, do not appear to be aware of, or know how to employ, specific strategies for enhancing comprehension.

Readers must be aware of the importance of monitoring their comprehension. A reader can only make the attempt to correct comprehension failure if there is an *awareness* that failure has occurred. First, students must become accustomed to "putting on the brakes" when something does not make sense. Then students must be able to make decisions about what to do about the comprehension failure. In order to make useful and efficient decisions about what to do to enhance comprehension or to rectify comprehension failure, students need to have a repertoire of text-processing strategies available from which they can choose. The student who comprehends well is the student who is actively involved in the reading process. According to

Stauffer (1969), reading is a thinking process that requires that the reader be an active participant. Teachers often ask the question "How can I help my students read with better comprehension?" We think that it is important that students be taught specific strategies that encourage and facilitate the active involvement of the reader in the comprehension process.

The specific strategies described in this chapter are referred to as text-processing strategies because they encourage the reader to focus on comprehension *during* the reading process. The four examples of text-processing strategies detailed in this chapter are *prediction*, *self-questioning*, *mental imagery*, and *rereading*. There are many strategies that skilled readers are known to employ while reading text; therefore, this list should not be considered exhaustive. The Guided Strategy Instruction procedure described in Chapter 2 is an explicit model that teachers can use to teach text-processing strategies.

These strategies encourage active participation on the part of the reader during the reading process. There is speculation that some children have difficulty comprehending what they read because they do not focus their concentration on the task. They do not put forth the sustained effort required for the complex task of comprehension. The examples of strategies for comprehending text presented in this chapter encourage both active participation and sustained effort during the reading process. The goal of comprehension instruction is for the student to possess *ownership* of a variety of text-processing strategies and to be able to determine how and when to implement the strategies to enhance comprehension of text.

PREDICTION

The prediction strategy involves students in making personal statements about what they believe will happen in a text passage based upon some bit of information, such as a title, picture, or paragraph. Prediction encourages students to activate prior knowledge and to take risks by piecing together their own prior knowledge and the information provided in the text to make predictions about the passage

The Prediction Process

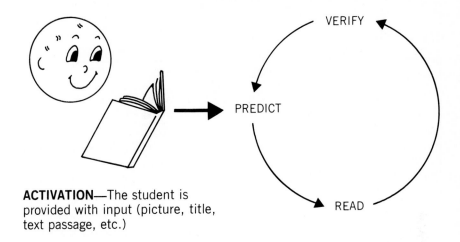

ACTIVATION—The student is provided with input (picture, title, text passage, etc.)

content. Engaging students in the prediction process encourages active participation in the comprehension process (Stauffer, 1969).

When modeling the prediction strategy using the think-aloud procedure it is important that the teacher model the continuous nature of the prediction process.

In modeling the prediction strategy the teacher might say something similar to the following:

> *Teacher*: Let me illustrate how the prediction strategy can help you read with better understanding. Here is a story that I have not read. The title of the story is *The Runner*. I want to read this story and understand what it is about. One thing that I can do to understand what I read is to make predictions about what I think might happen in the story. Making predictions will help me think more clearly about the story as I read it. I have read the title of the story and the story is about a runner. First, I want to think about what I know about runners. I already know that some people run for exercise and some people run in races. Now I am going to make some predictions based upon the title of the story and what I already know about runners.

(As the teacher thinks aloud, the predictions are recorded on the board.)

Teacher: I think this story will be about (1) a runner who is trying to win a race, or (2) a runner who is a secret messenger.

(The teacher now proceeds to read the text aloud to the group.)

THE RUNNER

I didn't cry when Grandpa died. Everyone else cried, but I just couldn't. I really don't know why. The newspapers were filled with articles about Grandpa and stories about his life from boyhood to his death. Most of all, there were stories about his fame. He had been a famous track star in his youth.

Teacher: Now that I have read the first paragraph of the story I know that my prediction about the runner trying to win a race is probably on target. I found out that Grandpa was a track star, and I know that people who run in track meets are trying to win a race or break a record of some kind. Now I'm going to predict that when I read more of the story I will find out why Grandpa was called a track star. I already know that some track runners run the mile and some specialize in the quarter-mile races. I also think I might find out whether Grandpa won any special races or prizes. I know that sometimes the winner of a race gets a special trophy and sometimes they may even win a lot of money. Now I will read the next section of the story to find out whether my predictions are on target.

The prediction strategy is cyclical in that it is a continuous process. Here are some things to keep in mind as the basic steps of the prediction process—*activation, prediction, reading,* and *verifying*—are being developed with students.

1. Activation. Initially, the reader is exposed to some basic bit of information relevant to the text passage in order to activate the prediction process. The teacher must decide, prior to the direct teaching of the prediction strategy, what aspect of the text passage or story is most appropriate for generating predictions. It might be the title of the selection, a particular picture or graphic presentation, or even a selected paragraph from the text. When the prediction process is to be activated by a selection from the text, the students are directed to read the selection, or for variety the teacher may read the selection aloud to the students.

2. *Prediction.* The reader makes predictions about what will happen based upon the text information and the reader's prior knowledge about the content. The teacher can encourage predictions by sharing with students the notion that there is no such thing as an incorrect prediction. A prediction is your best idea or guess about what is going to happen. Since a prediction is a guess, not all predictions that a person makes will be consistent with what happens in the text. A person who uses the prediction strategy effectively is a person who thinks about the passage information (the title, picture, paragraph, etc.) and then thinks about what he or she knows (prior knowledge) and based upon these two things makes a prediction about what the passage will be about. Using the think-aloud procedure, the teacher can model prediction questions, such as "What do I think this passage is going to be about?" "What kinds of things do I think I will learn from reading this selection?" or "What do I think is going to happen next?"

It is especially important that the teacher model the thinking process that is so essential to the effective use of the prediction strategy by verbalizing the process of *comparing the text information with prior knowledge* in order to generate text-relevant predictions. For example, the picture below might be used to activate predictions about a story that students are going to read. The teacher might say something like the following:

> *Teacher*: Today, we will be reading a new story, *My Friend Benji*. Open your books and look carefully at the picture on page 18. Decide what you think is happening here.

> *Teacher*: What do you already know about tigers? Based upon what you see in the picture and what you already know about tigers, what do you think is going to happen in this story?

In this example, the teacher has modeled the process of using the text information (what the students see in the picture) in conjunction with prior knowledge (what the students already know about tigers) to generate text-relevant predictions.

3. Reading. In this step the students read the text to determine the accuracy of the predictions that have been generated. Here the teacher might say something similar to the following:

> *Teacher*: Let's read to find out whether any of our predictions are on target.

4. Verifying. Now the reader compares the predictions (made during step 2) with the information gained from reading the passage. Each prediction can now be evaluated in light of what has been learned from the text. Referring to the predictions that are recorded on the board, the teacher can have students give evidence that the predictions have proven to be:

1. *True*, if there is support in the text for the prediction.
2. *False*, if there is support in the text for the contention that the prediction is not true.
3. *Questionable*, if there is no information to support either the relevance or the irrelevance of the prediction to the text. In these instances, further reading may provide evidence to make a judgment about the prediction.

To guide the discussion about the relevance of the predictions the teacher might ask questions like the ones below.

> *Teacher*: Let's discuss which of our predictions were on target, given the pages we have just read.

(Students give supporting information for the predictions that are confirmed.)

> *Teacher*: Are there some predictions here that, even though we don't know the answer yet, may be proven out as we read more of the story?

(Students give ideas and opinions.)

> *Teacher*: Were any of our predictions inaccurate for this story?

(Students provide supporting information.)

The teacher can code each prediction on the board as the discussion proceeds. Predictions that are verified as being on target can be checked or starred, those that prove to be incorrect or irrelevant to the text can be crossed out, and those that are still questionable can be marked with a question mark.

At this point new predictions are formulated based upon the information gained from the reading of the text, and the cyclical process continues. To encourage the generation of more refined predictions the teacher might say something like "Now that we have learned more about . . . (or now that we know that . . .), can we come up with some predictions about what will happen next?"

Students will profit from teacher-guided practice in using prediction as a comprehension strategy, however, having students apply the prediction strategy in their independent reading is a primary goal. When students engage in the prediction process, they are actively involved in the process of making sense of what they are reading.

SELF-QUESTIONING

Teaching students to use self-questioning as a comprehension strategy involves them in posing questions about the content of the text *during* the reading process. We know that good readers constantly engage in the process of posing questions about what they are reading and that these self-questions guide the reader in the search for understanding. Evidence suggests that training low-ability students to pose self-questions about what they are reading improves their comprehension performance significantly (Andre & Anderson, 1978–79).

There is a close relationship between the prediction and the self-questioning strategy. While both strategies engage students in posing questions, the self-questioning strategy involves students in posing content-specific questions about the text as opposed to the more general questions that typify the prediction strategy. The teacher might want to clarify the differences between the two strategies by discussing the fact that for some materials, such as narrative stories, it is sometimes more appropriate to try to predict what will happen. For other stories, and especially expository materials, it may be easier to ask specific self-questions. Sometimes it might depend upon which strategy the reader is most comfortable using. Obviously, both prediction and self-questioning can be used with a variety of materials.

Students may not understand why it is important for the reader to engage in self-questioning during reading. Some students may not have a sense of exactly how and when to engage in self-questioning. Teacher modeling, using the think-aloud procedure, can provide students with an example of how this strategy can be implemented during the reading process.

The teacher might introduce the self-questioning strategy with a rationale that goes something like this:

Teacher: Asking yourself specific questions about what you are reading can help you understand and remember.

(The teacher might then "think-aloud" using the self-questioning strategy.)

Teacher: Using the self-questioning strategy can help me understand and remember what I read. I am going to use the self-questioning strategy when I read this passage titled, *Sequoya*, to you. I will think-aloud so you can see how I use the self-questioning strategy while I read. I already have some specific questions about this passage just from reading the title:
1. Will this passage be about sequoia trees?
2. Will this passage be about the Sequoya Indians?
Now I'll read to see whether my questions are answered.

SEQUOYA

Sequoya, a Cherokee Indian, invented a system of writing. He was born in Tennessee. His family was very much respected among the Cherokee Indians for their understanding of tribal customs. Sequoya made friends with some English-speaking people. He became very interested in their way of communicating by writing. He decided to invent a system of writing for his own people.

Teacher: Now I know that the passage is about Sequoya, a Cherokee Indian, and I have other questions about the passage:

1. Why did Sequoya think that his people needed a system of writing?
2. Was it difficult to develop a system of writing?

Now I will read to see whether I find the answers to my questions.

It took Sequoya 12 years to complete the work on the writing system for the Cherokee Indians. Sequoya felt that it was important for the Cherokee people to record ancient tribal customs in a lasting form. That is why he worked for so long to develop a writing system for his people. The Cherokee nations used his system to produce books and newspapers in their own language. Thousands of the Cherokee Indians learned to read and to write in their own language.

Teacher: Now I know the answer to my question "Why did Sequoya think that his people needed a system of writing?" He wanted the Cherokee people to be able to record their tribal customs. I also found out something about my second question, "Was it difficult to develop a system of writing?" The text says that it took Sequoya 12 years to develop the writing system so it must have been both a difficult and time-consuming task. Now I have other questions:

1. What tribal customs were recorded by the Sequoyas?
2. Do the sequoia trees have anything to do with the Sequoya Indians?

I'll read now to see whether I find answers to these questions.

In this modeling example the teacher has illustrated the specific nature of self-questions and the continuous nature of the self-questioning strategy. Self-questioning engages the reader in continuously interacting with the text. During teacher-guided practice the teacher identifies the stopping points for posing questions and answering questions. The goal of having students use self-questioning independently means that ultimately the reader takes charge of determining stopping points for considering what has been read and for posing additional questions.

VISUAL IMAGERY

The old saying "A picture is worth a thousand words" may explain why visual imagery is a strategy that enhances reading comprehension.

When students make visual images, the "pictures" may provide the framework for organizing and remembering information. There is considerable evidence that comprehension and memory are increased when students employ visual imagery (Pressley, 1976; Gambrell & Bales, 1986). However, it appears that students do not spontaneously use visual imagery to enhance their comprehension (Gambrell & Bales, 1986). Students may not spontaneously use visual imagery as a strategy to facilitate comprehension because, for one reason, visual imagery is most frequently associated with esthetic appreciation of prose and is not directly taught as a specific comprehension strategy (Belcher, 1981). While visual imagery has been found to increase both listening and reading comprehension, it is clear that students need direct instruction in how and when to apply this specific strategy.

Below are suggested activities for teaching students to use visual imagery and some suggestions for encouraging students to use visual imagery as a specific reading comprehension strategy.

1. Inform students that making pictures in your mind can help you understand what a story or passage is about. Specific directions, depending upon whether the text is narrative or expository, may be helpful. For example, "Make pictures in your mind of the interesting characters in this story," "Make pictures in your mind about the things that happen in this story," or "Make a picture in your mind of our solar system." Using visual imagery in this manner encourages students to integrate information across text as they engage in the constructive processing of information.
2. Inform students that when something is difficult to understand it sometimes helps to try to make a picture in your mind. Using visual imagery can help students clarify meaning, and it encourages them to think about whether they are comprehending.
3. Encourage students to make visual images about stories or information they want to remember. Tell them that making pictures in your mind can help you remember. As a follow-up to story time or the silent reading of basal stories, have students think about the visual images they made and en-

courage them to use their images to help them retell the story to a partner (or as homework, to retell the story to a parent or sibling). This activity will help students realize the value of using visual imagery to enhance memory.

Since the research on visual imagery strongly suggests that students will employ visual imagery if directed to do so, but they do not spontaneously use the strategy, it seems important to provide adequate teacher-guided practice in the use of this strategy. In order to encourage the spontaneous use of this strategy many opportunities for students to use the strategy independently need to be provided. Here are some considerations to take into account when selecting materials to be used to encourage visual imagery:

1. For modeling and teacher-guided practice activities select brief passages of paragraph length.
2. Choose passages that are high in image-evoking quality.
3. Point out that not all text material is easy to visualize. Visual imagery may not be the best strategy to use if it is very difficult to make images about the passage; in these situations the reader should identify another strategy that would be helpful.

Teachers can take advantage of their students' natural ability to visualize and teach them to use the visual imagery strategy for enhancing memory and comprehension skills. With practice, students can learn to use visual imagery to enhance their reading comprehension.

REREADING

A commonly used strategy for enhancing comprehension is the very basic strategy of rereading (Olshavsky, 1976–77). Good readers frequently report that if they do not understand something, they go back and reread the passage. When the reader goes back to reread something that has not made sense there is a concentrated effort to engage in deeper processing in order to "make sense" out of what has been read.

This is such an obvious strategy that it might be overlooked, however, explicit instruction about *when* and *how* to use the rereading strategy may be beneficial to younger and less skilled readers. Many younger and less skilled readers may not be aware of the potential of this very basic comprehension strategy.

Teachers can introduce rereading as a reading comprehension strategy using the think-aloud procedure. First, the teacher would choose a difficult or ambiguous passage. While reading the passage the teacher would model comprehension failure by verbalizing about "miscomprehension" or "lack of comprehension." Then the teacher would say something like "That is not clear to me. I don't think I understand what the author is saying. One thing that I can do when I do not understand is go back and reread the passage again. This time I will reread the paragraph to see whether I understand more clearly what the author is trying to communicate."

Distortion of the meaning of text can occur for many reasons; for example, misreading a word, misinterpreting a phrase, or incorrect phrasing may result in comprehension failure. These are only a few examples of situations where rereading may be the most efficient strategy for repairing comprehension failure. To emphasize the usefulness of the rereading strategy the teacher might ask students to share situations where they encountered difficulty during the initial reading of the text, but were able to understand more clearly after rereading the text. Having students describe what caused their comprehension failure and give reasons *why* the rereading strategy was effective emphasizes the importance of being able to recognize comprehension failure when it occurs and being able to employ a specific strategy to resolve the failure.

CHAPTER SUMMARY

Students need to be aware of a variety of strategies they can employ *during* reading that will facilitate the comprehension process. In this chapter four strategies for comprehending text were presented: prediction, self-questioning, mental imagery, and rereading. Students can be taught to employ these strategies *during* text processing in order to enhance comprehension.

REFERENCES

Andre, M.E.D., & Anderson, T. H. (1978–79). The development and evaluation of a self-questioning study technique. *Reading Research Quarterly*, *14*, 605–623.

Belcher, V. (1981). Mental imagery in basal manuals. Unpublished manuscript. College Park, Md.: Reading Center, University of Maryland.

Gambrell, L. B., & Bales, R. J. (1986). Mental imagery and the comprehension monitoring performance of fourth and fifth grade poor readers. *Reading Research Quarterly*, *21*, 454–464.

Olshavsky, J. E. (1976–77). Reading as problem solving: An investigation of strategies. *Reading Research Quarterly*, *12*, 654–674.

Pressley, M. (1976). Mental imagery helps eight-year-olds remember what they read. *Journal of Educational Psychology*, *68*, 355–359.

Stauffer, R. G. (1969). *Directing reading maturity as a cognitive process*. New York.

Strategies for Enhancing Text Reorganization

4

To remember text information readers must be able to reorganize that information so that it has personal meaning for them. Except in the case of very short passages, readers cannot remember text information in the author's exact words. The author's ideas must be reorganized into a framework that readers think important. In fact, this is the only way that readers can remember information from text.

Students use different strategies to remember text information. But regardless of the strategy used, that strategy must always involve some type of text reorganization. If readers make personal reflections on how to tell others about an event, a television show, or a book that has been read, they realize that it is essential to report the essence of this information. They simply cannot remember each word and each detail. For example, if I were to discuss the events of a Big Ten football game with a friend, we'd be likely to reflect upon some outstanding plays, a great coaching decision, or a fine half-time show. We just could not remember all of the details of the game. Likewise, if we wanted to discuss James A. Michener's *Chesapeake*, we'd need to select the ideas from that book that seemed important to us. There is no way that we could remember all of Michener's ideas and certainly not all of his words. And, nobody would be interested in our verbatim account of that book, even if we could remember all of it.

Although everyone has his or her own way of reorganizing text, it is possible that some ways are not very efficient. We believe that it is desirable to provide Guided Strategy Instruction to teach several effective strategies to all readers. The ultimate purpose is for students to own these strategies so that they can use them whenever they think them appropriate. For the purposes of this text, we'll concentrate on four reorganization strategies:

- Think-links
- Personal outlining
- Retelling
- Summarizing

While there are many other strategies for text reorganization, these four represent techniques that students can learn to employ to enhance text comprehension and study skills. The only *rule* about text reorganization is that students must use some type of personal decision making to decide what is to be remembered. One strategy might suit one student, while another might be more effective for another student. A student might select a given strategy for a narrative passage and a different one for an expository passage. Our contention is that students should be taught various strategies so that they can employ an appropriate one, independent of teacher direction or guidance.

THINK-LINKS

Think-links involve the development of graphic configurations that represent important ideas and important details from the text that has been read (Lyman, Lopez, & Mindus, 1977). The notion that ideas are tied together in passages has led some educators to refer to think-links as "webs." In this book the terms *think-links* and *webs* refer to the same comprehension reorganization strategy.

Students often fail to notice how text information is linked. It is even possible that some of the reading comprehension instruction that they have focused upon details and unrelated bits of information. Instruction on the use of think-links can help students realize various ways that text information is related.

Think-link instruction is initiated through Guided Strategy Instruction (see Chapter 2). Most students, however, seem to develop the ability to use think-links independently after only a few lessons. An example of one type of think-link will be illustrated using the following story about a young boy, Matthew, and his dog Max.

Matthew loved Max and played with him every day. When Matthew went to school, Max would be very sad. Around 3:30 every day, Max would sit by the front door, waiting to welcome Matthew home. Then they would go out into the backyard and play catch with a tennis ball. Max never got tired of playing catch with Matthew.

One day Matthew had to stay after school to practice for a play. Max was waiting by the door at 3:30. By 3:45 Max began to whine. By 4:30 Max had become very upset and started to bark loudly. And then, at 4:45, Max's ears perked up as he heard the school bus stop in front of the house. His tail was wagging rapidly as he saw Matthew coming up the sidewalk. When Matthew's mother told him about how unhappy Max had been, Matthew's eyes swelled with tears. He took his friend out back right away and played catch with him for an hour.

That night Matthew's parents permitted Max to break a house rule, which was: No dogs in bed! Max slept all night at Matthew's feet and Matthew woke up several times to hear a soft cooing sound coming from Max. In the morning Matthew wondered how he could tell Max that he could not stay in the bed tonight. It turned out he didn't need to. The house rule had been broken and was never to be enforced again.

Teachers can help students learn to use think-links as a comprehension strategy as follows. After silently reading a short story, like the one above, the teacher can start by explaining the use of think-links to the students.

Teacher: Today we are going to think about the story we have just read by using character think-links.

Then the teacher can model the development of a character think-link using the think-aloud procedure.

Teacher: One major character in this story was Matthew. So I'm going to write Matthew's name in this circle on our chart paper.

Dr. David Williams

Then I'm going to write some words above the circle that might be used to explain how Matthew felt at different times in the story.

Now the teacher can start to develop a think-link by writing one of the words on a line coming from the circle.

Teacher: I think I'll write "guilty" on this line and try to think of any times during the story that Matthew might have felt guilty. Let me think—he might have felt guilty about coming home from school late. I'll write that thought here and draw a circle around it. Can anyone think of another time that Matthew might have felt guilty? If so, I'll write your thought in another circle at the end of the "guilty" line.

The teacher continues, placing another word on another line and helping students to think about ideas that might be appropriate for that word. The finished link might look something like the following:

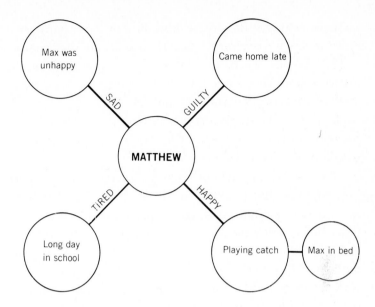

A think-link could then be developed using Max as the character. That think-link might look something like the following:

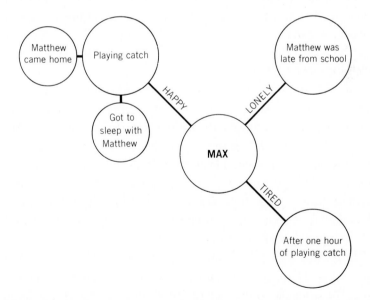

After several guided lessons, teachers might want to permit the students to try developing their own think-links. After reading a story the teacher might develop a think-link on one character and permit the students to develop the second one on another character.

Think-links can be developed from stories such as the one illustrated above. They serve as text reorganizers. Once developed, they can be used as preparation materials for oral and written reports. Each stem of the think-link can become the material to be used in a paragraph. This helps even very young learners to understand the nature of the paragraph.

Think-links can also be used as "preparation for reading" activities. Suppose that the story to be read was about a family living in Hawaii. To facilitate reading comprehension, the teacher develops a think-link using student prior knowledge for the information to go into it. The teacher might develop the think-link by placing Hawaii in the middle and using words like *people*, *agriculture*, *recreation*, and *cities* as stem words. Some students might have a good bit of information about Hawaii, having been there, seen television programs about it, or read a book about it. Those students could contribute their information to the think-link. Those without information about Hawaii benefit because they will be learning from their peers' contributions. Then, after reading the story about a family who live in Hawaii, the class can go back to the think-link to determine (1) what might be added and (2) what might need to be changed to make the think-link more accurate.

Think-links can also be used to stimulate thinking about special events, such as field trips, science experiments, cooking activities, motion pictures, and school assemblies. Using think-links in this manner captures the special event with students' thoughts and in a graphic way. By saving these special events on think-links, a student's memory of an event can be improved. And students can use the think-links, of course, to write about or discuss the events. Think-links also make very interesting room decorations that carry meaning through students' language contributions.

Think-links can take many graphic forms. The character think-links that were used in our initial illustration are only one of those forms. For example, a teacher might want to compare likenesses and differences between some story characters. Such a think-link might be developed as follows:

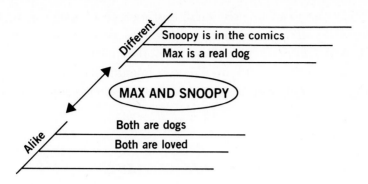

Or a teacher might want to use social studies or science as the subject of the think-link. The following think-link might serve well as a culminating activity for a unit on Gettysburg:

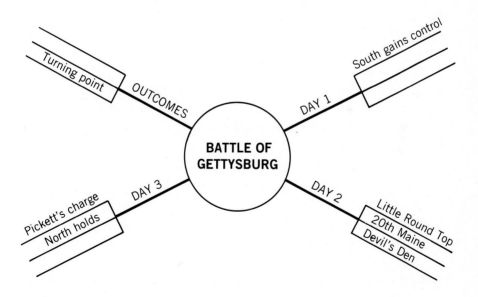

The teacher could ask the students what they thought they had learned. Either the teacher or the students could provide the stem words. The resulting think-link presents the students with a graphic–language display of their learning. And, as stated before, they can be used for oral and written reports on the topics that have been studied.

Think-links can be very small and focused or they can be quite extensive. Some teachers start a think-link one day and let students add to it day after day. They can take up an entire chalkboard or an entire wall in the classroom. One can imagine how a think-link following a baseball world series or a hostage crisis could develop for days.

PERSONAL OUTLINES

As students mature in their reading abilities, graphic configurations might be less necessary as a way to reorganize text. One way to move students from think-links to another way of personal reorganization of text is through the use of personal outlines.

Personal outlines call for teachers to start with *personal* questions about what has been read. They might ask students what *they thought* was most interesting or most important about what they just read. Since the teacher's question is a personal one, each student's answer must be viewed as acceptable. To show acceptance of a student's response without approval or disapproval, record it on a chalkboard or on chart paper. Recording the response is an accepting activity. If a student says, "I thought it was a boring story," that response is recorded and accepted, not judged to be correct or incorrect.

When students have difficulty answering personal questions, the teacher can once again model for the students.

> *Teacher*: I thought it was interesting that Max knew the time of day at 3:30. Does your dog know the time of day?

Then the teacher records that thought for students to read. There is a problem with modeling answers to personal questions: Students tend to believe that the modeled answer is the right one. The teacher must quickly ask, "Who has another idea of an interesting part of this story?"

Once all of the students' responses to the personal questions have been recorded, the teacher can ask the students to think about all of those responses and decide which one they would now choose.

> *Teacher*: Someone else's idea might seem better than your first response.

Teachers need to explain to students that it is all right to change their minds. Not only is it all right; it is often the best thing to do. Initially, many students seem reluctant to make this type of move. In those cases, the teacher again models by thinking aloud.

> *Teacher*: Well, I thought it was most interesting that Max knew the time of day, but Jennifer's notion that Max beat the house rule of no sleeping in bed is now my favorite choice. And Sharon's notion that Matthew's parents were very understanding also interests me. Perhaps there is more than one interesting idea in this story. Who wants to make another choice?

Once everyone has chosen an interesting idea, the teacher hands out a form that looks like this:

1. _____
   Interesting idea
   a. _____
      Supporting detail
   b. _____
      Supporting detail
   c. _____
      Supporting detail
2. _____
   Interesting idea
   a. _____
      Supporting detail
   b. _____
      Supporting detail
   c. _____
      Supporting detail

The students are now instructed to write their most interesting idea on line 1. Then they are to find as many supporting details as they can and write them on lines a, b, and c. They might find only one supporting detail, but they could find as many as three or more. This step is repeated for the second interesting idea. Teachers will probably need to model this selection of supporting details step (thinking aloud as they do so), since many students might have little experience in doing this.

When completed, each student has a personal outline of the story or text. The outlines are personal because each student made a personal decision about what to include. Are they accurate? Maybe, or maybe not—but that is where instruction can start. Accurate outlines can be reinforced and discussed with alternatives for further activities, such as writing and more student discussion. Less than accurate outlines will need further teacher feedback.

Teacher feedback during these lessons is very important. If a student responds, "I love my dog," that student will find no support for that interesting idea, however good it might be. In such cases, the teacher must ask the student, "Well, I love my dog, too, but this story did not address any ideas about your dog. Whose dog was it? What is your dog's name? How is your dog like or not like Max?" These kinds of teacher questions help to clarify students' responses to personal questions and personal outlines.

There are some real benefits to instruction through the use of personal outlines. Students tend to remember their personal outlines because they *are* personal and have meaning for them. Students can use personal outlines when doing topical research. Teachers know that topical research reports often result in no more than a reading or writing of an account from some resource reference. Students are bored by this type of reporting, and the reporter often does not know what the report means.

Outlining seems to be a difficult skill for some students to learn. Starting outlining instruction with personal questions can facilitate student learning. Outlining is, of course, one of the major study skills, involving the reorganization of a message, whether oral or written.

RETELLING

Another strategy for helping students with the reorganization of text is that of retelling. Retelling is often used by teachers as an assessment of text comprehension. Retelling is seldom used, however, as a strategy for enhancing the comprehension of text. One reason for this may be that retelling as an individual activity requires a great deal of time. There are, however, very practical and efficient ways of teaching retelling as a reading comprehension strategy.

Research suggests that retelling is a learned skill that facilitates literal and interpretive comprehension. There has been ample evidence that verbal rehearsal enhances learning (Craik & Watkins, 1973; Ornstein & Naus, 1978). Only recently, however, have educators begun to take a look at the relationship between verbal rehearsal and reading comprehension (Gambrell, Pfeiffer, & Wilson, 1985). Evidence suggests that practice in using retelling following silent reading enhances reading comprehension, even the ability of students to answer both literal and interpretive questions. One concern of teachers has been that since students are often paired for retelling they might be engaged in retelling inaccurate information. Research findings suggest, however, that students rarely if ever retell inaccurate information (Gambrell, Koskinen, & Kapinus, 1985). It might be useful for teachers to think of ways to help students gain the experience for the effective retelling of text. We will suggest a few.

1. Teachers can model retelling by taking a few minutes to retell a portion of a story. This modeling could include the retelling of exciting events that might interest the students. Teachers can also model accurate sequencing while retelling a story. They can use the think-aloud strategy when trying to recall what happened next in the story.
2. Teachers can retell a portion of an event and ask the students to finish the retelling. For example, the teacher might retell all but the exciting ending of a story. Students can be given the opportunity to give their retellings of the ending.

3. Teachers can ask a few students to recall what they thought was the most important or interesting event in the story. In another lesson other students can be given a chance at retelling what they thought was most important or interesting. Such retelling is a very personal opportunity for students to experience this important strategy. They are not expected to retell the entire story so they can concentrate on doing a good job recalling a small portion of the story. Those students not involved with the retelling can listen and learn from their classmates.

4. Teachers can easily pair students for the purpose of retelling important or interesting story events to their partner. If the students are seated at a table for their reading instruction, the teacher can easily listen in on different students' retellings. In this way the teacher can determine which students need more guidance in selecting events to retell or in organizing their retellings.

5. During independent study time when the teacher is not directly involved with group instruction, teachers can call students for private conferences during which they can retell portions of stories.

Retelling involves students in the process of relating one part of the text to another. It involves students drawing upon their prior knowledge in order to know what is worth retelling. It is a holistic approach to reading comprehension since the retelling needs to begin and end with logical chunks of information.

SUMMARIZING

One of the life skills most frequently called upon is that of summarizing. In classrooms, students are often asked to tell what a passage or a story was about. Every day people engage in summarizing what they have read or heard as they tell, for example, about newspaper articles they have read, movies they have seen, and books they have read. Summarizing is an important text-reorganization skill for students to use to enhance their reading comprehension (Taylor, 1982). Summarizing is a form of retelling, but it is more focused and more concise than the retelling that was just discussed.

Several steps are involved in helping students learn to become effective summarizers. Students must understand that a summary tells the key ideas of a passage. A summary does not contain any minor details. A summary is brief, but it must include the central ideas of the passage. Students need to be able to discriminate between good summaries and poor summaries. To help students distinguish the features of good summaries the teacher can present passages and samples of summaries. Students can discuss whether a given summary is appropriate.

The teacher has selected the following brief passage to use to demonstrate the difference between good and poor summaries.

THREE FRIENDS

The three were growing tired from their arduous journey. Soon they would have to cross a raging river. It was wide and deep. They were not sure they would be able to swim across.

The smaller boy plunged into the swirling water and yelled for the others to follow him. The larger boy jumped into the water. Although he was weak, he managed to struggle to the opposite bank.

The third boy was afraid and remained on the bank alone. He just stood there, trembling with fright. The younger boy swam back toward him and yelled, "Jump, I'll help you." Finally the frightened boy jumped in and began to swim toward his friend.

At that moment something bad happened. An old beaver dam from upstream broke. The water came rushing downstream hurling a large log toward the two boys.

Following the silent reading of this passage the teacher can present some sample summaries. The teacher might say, "Read these three summaries of the passage we just read. Identify the best summary, and decide why it is an appropriate summary and why the other summaries do not meet the criteria for a good summary."

Summary A

Three boys, tired from a long journey, were trying to cross a river. The river was wide and deep. Two boys started to swim the river but one boy did not want to try it. Finally, the frightened boy jumped in. At that moment something bad happened. The dam broke just as the two boys started to swim across the river.

Summary B

Three boys were trying to cross a river. Two boys started to swim across the river all right, but one boy would not try it. The younger boy returned to help his friend. Just as they were swimming across the river together, a dam broke, hurling a log toward them.

Summary C

Three friends were trying to swim across a river. Two of them got into trouble.

When the students have finished reading the three summaries, the teacher can lead a discussion about which summary is most appropriate and why. Some of the points for discussion could be:

Summary A is *not* the best summary because it contains a lot of details that might be best left out. It almost retells the passage.

Summary C is *not* the best summary because it does not contain the important ideas from the passage.

Summary B is a *good* summary because it does fit the criteria for a good summary. It includes the major ideas but is brief enough not to include minor details from the passage.

Following the discussion, the students should be able to generate the features of a good summary:

1. A good summary contains the major ideas of the passage.
2. A good summary is brief.
3. A good summary does not contain very many details.

When students can identify the characteristics of a good summary, the teacher can have them generate their own summaries of both expository and narrative texts. It is important to have students develop summaries of brief passages in the beginning and then move to larger amounts of text as they become more proficient in generating summaries.

Students should be encouraged to summarize when they study or when they want to remember what they have read. Taylor (1982) found that having students write one-sentence summaries of what they have read resulted in increased reading comprehension. Students can use the summarizing strategy when pausing during silent reading to summarize to themselves about what they have read. Or they might write brief summaries about what they think was important to remember. Summarizing is an important text-reorganization strategy for readers to use.

CHAPTER SUMMARY

While students obviously must develop some ways for the reorganization of text that they have read if they want to retain any information, some strategies work better than others. This chapter presents four that work very well for most students. Each of these strategies needs a certain amount of direct teacher instruction and supervised follow-up to develop independence or ownership for the students. Teachers will need to decide how much of each strategy their students will need and when they will need it.

REFERENCES

Craik, F. I., & Watkins, M. J. (1973). The role of rehearsal in short-term memory. *Journal of Verbal Learning and Verbal Behavior*, *12*, 599–607.

Gambrell, L., Pfeiffer, W., & Wilson, R. (1985). The effects of retelling upon reading comprehension and recall of text information. *Journal of Educational Research*, *78*, 216–220.

Gambrell, L. B., Koskinen, P. S., & Kapinus, B. (December, 1985). Retelling as an instructional strategy for elementary school children. Paper presented at the National Reading Conference, San Diego, Calif.

Lyman, F., Lopez, C., & Mindus, A. (1977). *Language Arts Guide*. Howard County Board of Education, Clarksville, Md.

Ornstein, P. A., & Naus, M. J. (1978). Rehearsal processes in children's memory. In P. A. Ornstein (Ed.), *Memory development in children*. Hillsdale, N.J.: Erlbaum.

Taylor, B. M. (1982). A summarizing strategy to improve middle grade students' reading and writing skills. *The Reading Teacher*, *36*, 202–205.

Approaches to 5
Reading Comprehension
Instruction

When planning for reading comprehension instruction, the first consideration is the approach to be used. By *approach* we mean the general instructional procedure. The approach selected may be very teacher directed, very student directed, or some combination of teacher and student direction.

The selection of approaches may be based on one or several of the following factors that teachers will need to consider:

1. Teacher preference. Teachers often have preferences for one approach over another. These preferences might be based on their past experiences, their teacher education training, or some professional literature they have studied.
2. School policy. A principal, a supervisor, or a school superintendent might expect a given approach to be used. Teachers employed in these schools are expected to use the approach that has been indicated as a school priority. Most school systems, however, would prefer to have teachers use approaches with which they are most comfortable.
3. Materials available for instruction. Many teachers find themselves limited in their choice of approach because of the type of material that is available for comprehension

instruction. This is especially true for teachers who do not feel well prepared to teach reading and therefore rely heavily upon commercially prepared teacher's guides.

4. Team decisions. Some schools have teachers working in teams. These teams might agree to use a common approach, even though that approach might not be the first choice of all of the team members.

5. Research. Some teachers might choose a given approach because of research that they have read about or conducted themselves.

6. Student needs. Teachers might believe that a given approach is better for their students because of their view of student needs. For example, some teachers might believe that their students need a lot of very direct instruction and therefore choose an approach on the side of the continuum that calls for teacher control.

7. Teacher needs. Some teachers need to feel that the students have a lot of controls over their learning, just as other teachers feel that *they* need to have that control.

While there are surely other factors that enter into a decision to choose one approach over another, the seven suggested above seem to be the major factors that influence teachers' decisions. One quickly realizes that teachers might be in situations in which they have no control about which approach to use. While this can easily cause much teacher frustration, we want to remind teachers that they have many instructional decisions to make about reading comprehension instruction (that is one of the major purposes for this book). For example, teachers can use a variety of instructional strategies, regardless of the approach being used (see Chapters 3, 4, 6, and 7). They can use a variety of supplemental materials for instruction (see Chapters 9 and 11). They can base their instruction on assessments they have made (see Chapter 11). And they can vary their instructional strategies for students with special needs (see Chapter 8).

We do not want to suggest that the selection of an approach to reading instruction is unimportant, only that teachers have a lot of important decisions to make about reading comprehension instruction. And they can make those decisions using any of the approaches.

OVERVIEW OF MAJOR APPROACHES

We assume that persons using this book either have had a basic course in reading or are already experienced teachers of reading. This assumption leads us to believe that our readers are already aware of the basic approaches to reading comprehension instruction and that a detailed explanation of the various approaches is not needed. On the chance that our assumptions are incorrect, we provide an overview of the major approaches to comprehension instruction with a reference for those who desire more information. The reader should understand that entire books have been written on each of these approaches, and numerous articles have appeared in the literature on each. Therefore, this overview is designed to remind readers of the options that are available, not to provide a detailed step-by-step guide for their use.

1. The Directed Reading Activity (DRA)

This approach is used by most of the commercial teacher's guides developed for use with basal readers. It involves much teacher control. The teacher

- Prepares the students for reading by establishing purposes for reading, introducing new vocabulary, and setting a background for the text to be read.
- Directs the students to the silent reading of the text.
- Stimulates discussion by means of teacher-generated questions.
- Directs rereading, oral or silent, to check on comprehension.
- Provides skills and enrichment activities.

The primary reference concerning the DRA is Betts, 1946.

2. The Directed Reading–Thinking Activity (DRTA)

This approach to comprehension instruction was developed to allow for more student control by introducing the notion of student prediction as a desirable element in comprehension instruction. Most commercial teacher's guides have aspects of the DRTA in them for teacher use.

- The teacher uses various aspect of the text (pictures, story titles, first paragraph, or student prior knowledge) to encourage student predictions about what might be about to occur. Teachers do not set purposes; students do. Teachers do not introduce new vocabulary unless it is very unusual. Students are expected to use the context, their prior knowledge, and their word-attack skills to deal with new words.
- Students read to check their predictions. It does not matter whether they were accurate. In fact, many very good stories are written to surprise the reader.
- Once the first predictions have been checked, new predictions are formed and the reader continues in this manner through the passage. This step can be very teacher directed or very student directed. That is, the teacher can have all students read the first two pages and then hold a discussion about their predictions. Or the students can read to check predictions, form new ones, and read on.
- The teacher directs a discussion about predictions and checks student predictions.
- Students reread, orally or silently, to verify their checks on their predictions and possibly on the predictions of others.
- The teacher provides skill and enrichment activities. New vocabulary found in the text is discussed and reinforced at this time.

In the DRTA approach the students make more decisions than they do in the DRA; at least they are in more control of the decisions they make. Most teacher's guides use some aspects of the DRTA as suggestions for instruction. The basic citation for the DRTA is Stauffer, 1981.

3. The Language Experience Approach (LEA)

Some reading authorities believe that the stories in basal readers are not very appropriate for beginning readers or for students experiencing difficulty with the reading comprehension process. They argue that these stories provide a poor match with the background knowledge and language of the readers. LEA, therefore, asks teachers to let students develop their own stories from experiences in their lives that have real and recent meanings.

- The teacher provides a common experience for the students: a field trip, a science experiment, a playground incident, or a story that has been shared.
- The teacher leads a discussion to generate language about this common experience. During this discussion key words or phrases can be written on the chalkboard or on chart paper.
- The teacher then leads the students in a discussion designed to recreate the experience in their own language. As the students contribute their ideas, the teacher writes them on the board or on chart paper. Some teachers place student names or initials after each student's contribution as a reminder of which students contributed which comment.
- The teacher then reads each comment to be certain that it is an accurate statement of what each student meant to contribute. Changes can be made to make the statements as accurate as possible. Students then read their own contributions, and this is followed by the entire group's reading each contribution. The teacher encourages the students to read their contributions just as they contributed them, that is, as close as possible to speech.
- The teacher encourages the students to select words from the story that they want to place in their word bank. The teacher writes these words on word cards (or the students do this if they can), and the students file the cards in their word banks.
- The teacher makes copies of the language experience story

so that all students can have a copy. The teacher can have
the students use these stories for reading practice or skill
activities, just as the students would use stories from prepared materials. These stories can be placed in a folder for
future reading activities.

LEA is a very attractive approach to both initial instruction and
remedial instruction. It has gained wide acceptance, especially in the
primary grades. LEA is also a natural approach for teachers to use
to help students develop creative writing activities. Once students
understand that they can use their language to develop stories, they
can start to write their own stories. Teachers should encourage any
students to write stories without fear of misspelling words. Spelling

errors can be corrected and used as a learning experience for the students. The basic citation here is Hall, 1981.

4. Individualized Reading

Individualized reading is an approach that uses student selection of reading materials (Veatch, 1978). These materials can be trade books, library books, magazines, or newspapers. Student selection involves interest in the topic of the material to be read. The topic of the book, the title of the story, or someone else's recommendation might be what triggers a selection. Obviously, the students are thinking about obtaining meaning and not about skill development or about satisfying someone else. Once the student starts to read, he or she might find the material too difficult or boring. When this happens, other reading material can be selected.

The students select what they want to read, record that choice in a log maintained by the teacher, and start to read for information and pleasure. The teacher sets conference times with all of the students. These conferences occur every couple of days. During the conference the students share their understanding of the reading material with the teacher. Both the students and the teacher can ask questions about what has been read to clarify understanding.

During the conference the teacher might discover that attention needs to be given to some aspect of vocabulary development or comprehension. If several students have a similar need, a small group can be temporarily formed to receive instruction. Most of the time, however, the students are involved in reading interesting material for their own purposes.

Veatch (1986) notes that these types of reading materials are written by creative artists, not by professional educators. She adds that they contain the best and most readable English of any materials available for reading comprehension instruction. Her notion is that personal commitment on the part of the learner is the key factor for success in an individualized reading program.

Combining Approaches

Most teachers are aware of the approaches discussed above. They have heard about them in classes and read about them in the literature on reading instruction. It is our observation, however, that many teachers seem to select one approach and stay with it all year long. While this might be comfortable for the teacher, it has the potential of being boring for the students. If the teacher chooses the DRTA as the preferred approach, it need not be the only approach. It could be supplemented with individualized reading a couple of days each week. It could be combined with LEA periodically. At times the teacher might feel more comfortable using the DRA format when certain teacher purposes seem to be important. For example, a teacher could use a DRA or a DRTA on Monday, Wednesday, and Friday and a LEA on Tuesday and Thursday.

We suggest that teachers become skilled in the use of each of these approaches and use whichever of them that is appropriate. The choice is really a matter of how much teacher direction is needed to meet the purposes of comprehension instruction.

CHAPTER SUMMARY

Teachers are encouraged to be familiar with the options available to them regarding the basic approaches to reading comprehension instruction. They also need to think about the reasons for using a given approach. A combination of approaches seems to be in the best interests of most of the students. Within each approach the teacher can use a variety of comprehension instructional strategies.

REFERENCES

Betts, E. (1946). *Foundations of Reading Instruction*. New York: American Book.

Hall, M. A. (1981). *Teaching Reading as a Language Experience*, 4th ed. Columbus, Ohio: Merrill.

Stauffer, R. (1981). *Teaching Reading as a Thinking Process*. New York: Harper & Row.

Veatch, J. (1978). *Reading in the Elementary School*, 2nd ed. New York: Wiley.

Veatch, J. (1986). "Teaching without texts." *Journal of Clinical Reading*, 2:1, 32–35.

Enhancing Comprehension Through Vocabulary Development

6

Knowledge of vocabulary, along with basic comprehension strategies, is the key to understanding both spoken and written language.
—Johnson and Pearson, 1984

Vocabulary knowledge has long been accepted as an integral component of reading comprehension. A major goal of comprehension instruction should be the expansion of students' knowledge of words and their meanings. Reading is an easy task if students are familiar with the words in a text; however, reading is a difficult task if the words encountered in the text are confusing or unknown (Johnson & Pearson, 1984).

DECISION MAKING FOR VOCABULARY INSTRUCTION

The total time allowed to reading instruction in the classroom is limited, and only a small portion of that time is typically devoted to vocabulary instruction. It is therefore essential that the most be made of the time devoted to enhancing vocabulary knowledge. In order to provide effective vocabulary instruction, Stahl (1986) suggests that the teacher address the following questions:

1. What words are to be taught?
2. Will the student be able to get the meanings of the words from context?
3. How thoroughly will the words need to be taught?
4. How much does the student know about the words?

What words are to be taught? Many time a basal series or a content textbook will have a list of vocabulary words that are to be introduced by the teacher. Often this list of words is extensive and would require a large portion of the total time allotted to reading instruction to be thoroughly taught. A first step in narrowing the list to the words that are most important for teacher-directed instruction would be to analyze each word in terms of the following criteria:

- Is the word critical to understanding the text?
- Is the word one that the student is likely to encounter again and again?

If the answer is "no" to both questions, the word is one that might be likely to be dropped from the instructional list (Stahl, 1986). Those words that are critical for understanding the text and words that will be frequently encountered in text should be given the highest priority in terms of inclusion in teacher-directed vocabulary instruction.

Will the student be able to get the meanings of the words from context? Sometimes a word is well defined in the context of the passage, which will enable the student to determine the meaning independently. However, in content textbooks, and to some extent in basal materials, authors will use a word and *assume* that the student knows the meaning of the word. If the word is well defined in the text, the word might be dropped from the instructional list. If the word is critical to text comprehension and the meaning is not revealed in context, the word should be included in teacher-directed vocabulary instruction.

How thoroughly will the words have to be taught? Sometimes words may be unfamiliar but the student may have the concept for a word that is similar to the unknown word. For example, the student may not know the word *bungling* but may know the word *clumsy* and have a firm understanding of the concept underlying this word. Words that are not in the student's reading vocabulary (such as *bungling*) but represent concepts that are relatively close to known words (*clumsy*) can be taught relatively easily by establishing the connection with known words and providing examples of use in context (Stahl, 1986). Other unfamiliar words may represent concepts that are not easily established, such as *democracy* and *citizenship*. When this is the case, more thorough instruction will be needed.

How much does the student know about the words? According to Dale and O'Rourke (1971), what a student knows about a given word may be classified according to three categories:

- totally known
- partially known
- totally unknown

A word that is *totally known* is one whose meaning is easily and instantly recognized. There are great numbers of words that every student "almost" knows, that is, words that are *partially known*. The student may have seen the word somewhere before, might recognize some part of the word (prefix, root, suffix), might recognize the word but not the meaning in a particular context, or might not recognize the word but be able to derive the meaning from context. In all these situations the student possesses partial but incomplete word knowledge. Many of these words may be easy for the student to learn through context alone and may require only minimal teacher-directed instruction. A word that is *totally unknown* is one that is totally unfamiliar to the student in every respect. Words that are totally unknown and are important for the student to know in order to read with strong understanding are the most crucial for inclusion in teacher-directed vocabulary instruction.

According to Graves and Prinn (1986) there is no one best method of teaching reading vocabulary. Different methods of teaching words are appropriate in different circumstances. The tasks students face in learning words will vary according to their level of knowledge of the words and the word meanings and will depend to a large extent upon how thoroughly the students need to know the words. For these reasons each method of teaching vocabulary will have costs and benefits.

GUIDELINES FOR
VOCABULARY INSTRUCTION

1. Vocabulary instruction should help students relate new vocabulary to their background knowledge. Instruction that relates new words to existing knowledge structures provides students with a basis for successfully incorporating the new words into their reading vocabulary (Eeds & Cockrum, 1985). Students should be active in creating connections between what they already know and new vocabulary so that the new vocabulary becomes personally meaningful. In this way the students' understanding of the new vocabulary is enhanced in ways that lead to increased reading comprehension (Carr & Wixson, 1986).

2. Vocabulary instruction should help students develop elaborated word knowledge. Vocabulary instruction should help students develop word knowledge that goes beyond knowing a simple definition or knowing a word in a single context (Johnson & Pearson, 1984). According to Stahl (1986), when a person "knows" a word, he or she can be thought of as having two types of knowledge about the word: definitional and contextual information.

Definitional information about a word is knowledge of the logical relations between the word and other known words. There are a variety of ways in which definitional information can be provided, such as through definitions, synonyms, antonyms, prefixes, suffixes, and roots (Stahl, 1986). In the sentence, "A gossip is a person who engages in idle talk that is based on groundless rumor," the definition of *gossip* as a noun is explicitly stated. In the following sentences definitional information is provided through the use of a synonym: "Ann was so dejected over the loss. She looked totally disheartened as she walked back to her room." The word *dejected* is defined by the use of the synonym *disheartened* in the second sentence.

Contextual information can be defined as "knowledge of the core concept the word represents and how that core concept is changed in different contexts" (Stahl, 1986). The word *run*, for example, means something slightly different when one makes a home "run," when one has a "run" in a pair of hose, and when one decides to "run" for office. Contextual information is derived from exposure to a word in context, usually a sentence; however, for some concrete words a picture or demonstration could provide contextual information.

For the purpose of enhancing elaborated word knowledge it is important that both definitional and contextual information be provided for vocabulary words. Research suggests that effective vocabulary instruction provides for a balance between definitional and contextual information in instructional activities (Stahl & Fairbanks, 1986).

3. Vocabulary instruction should provide for active student involvement in learning new vocabulary. There is ample research support for the contention that vocabulary instruction is more effective when students are actively involved in the construction of meaning through interactive processes rather than in memorizing definitions or synonyms (Beck, Perfetti, & McKeown, 1982; Stahl, 1983). The notion of active student involvement in learning is related to the "depth of processing" theory proposed by Craik and Lockhart (1972), which suggests that expending more of one's mental effort will result in greater learning. According to Carr and Wixson (1986), one feature that distinguishes active instructional approaches from other approaches is the extent to which the activities are student-directed as opposed to teacher-directed. When students are more deeply and actively involved in processing information through discussion and application activities, that information is more likely to be remembered than is information that has been processed in a shallow fashion.

4. Vocabulary instruction should help students develop independent strategies for acquiring new vocabulary. Teacher-directed vocabulary instruction should focus upon language generalizations and strategies that students will be able to use independently to increase their reading vocabularies (Johnson & Pearson, 1984).

Because of the enormous number of words an efficient reader

needs to understand, it is important for students to learn how to learn the meanings of new words *independently*. According to Carr and Wixson (1986), students should be aware of a variety of methods for acquiring word meanings; they should be able to monitor their level of understanding of new vocabulary and to change or modify strategies for deriving the meaning of new words if comprehension is not forthcoming.

5. *Vocabulary instruction should help students learn to value word knowledge.* Graves (in press) contends that if students do not come to value word knowledge truly, there is little chance that they will seriously care about learning new words or using words with precision. Teachers can and should serve as role models who demonstrate an interest and concern for word knowledge. Teachers can influence students by using clear, descriptive, interesting, and precise vocabulary. They can point out the interesting and exceptional use of words in the speech and writing that students encounter in the classroom. Teachers can share interesting facts about words and encourage students to become word "collectors." Helping students develop the motivation and desire to acquire new vocabulary is the very heart of vocabulary development (Ruddell, 1986).

INSTRUCTIONAL STRATEGIES FOR ENHANCING READING VOCABULARY

Teacher-directed vocabulary lessons should be offered on a regular basis. Research indicates that direct, planned vocabulary instruction is more effective than incidental learning for acquisition of specific vocabulary and for reading comprehension (Beck, Perfetti, & McKeown, 1982; Jenkins, Stein, & Wysocki, 1984; Nelson-Herber, 1986). This does not mean that the alert teacher cannot take advantage of opportunities to promote vocabulary growth in informal ways. In fact, exposing students to a print-rich environment should be a high priority, to afford many opportunities for the incidental learning of vocabulary. There is substantial evidence that students acquire much of their vocabulary knowledge through incidental learning (Jenkins, Stein, & Wysocki, 1984; Nagy, Herman, & Anderson, 1985), however, it is important that vocabulary instruction be offered on a regular basis. Students will meet with greater success when vocabulary instruction is based on a logical and systematic plan rather than on incidental, unplanned instruction.

In the following section instructional examples are provided for each of the five guidelines for vocabulary instruction:

1. Vocabulary instruction should help students relate new vocabulary to their background knowledge.
2. Vocabulary instruction should help students develop elaborated word knowledge.
3. Vocabulary instruction should provide for active student involvement in learning new vocabulary.
4. Vocabulary instruction should help students develop independent strategies for acquiring new vocabulary.
5. Vocabulary instruction should help students learn to value word knowledge.

One vocabulary development activity may incorporate features of a number of the guidelines and, in fact, some of the more effective activities will embody all the guidelines. An awareness of the guidelines for vocabulary instruction and the examples presented in this section should provide a starting point for teachers to develop instruction for the purpose of improving students' vocabulary knowledge and reading comprehension.

1. Relating New Vocabulary to Background Knowledge

One feature of effective vocabulary instruction is that it helps students relate new vocabulary to their prior knowledge. Students learn more readily and motivation is increased when vocabulary instruction is personally meaningful (Carr & Wixson, 1986). The *context-repetition procedure* and the *definition/example word cards* encourage students to relate new vocabulary to their own background of experiences.

CONTEXT-REPETITION PROCEDURE

In this procedure students are given a brief passage in which the new vocabulary word is used repeatedly in a defining context (Gipe, 1980). After reading the passage, students are asked to respond in writing to a question designed to encourage them to use the new vocabulary word based upon their personal experiences.

THE GUIDING LIGHT

It was hard to see the *beacon* in the thick fog. We knew we could get lost without the *beacon* to guide us. A *beacon* is a light that helps guide you or warn you of danger.

Where have you seen a *beacon* that is a warning sign?

I saw a beacon on top of a lighthouse on the eastern shore of Maryland.

DEFINITION/EXAMPLE WORD CARDS

This strategy makes use of individual word cards for encouraging students to associate their background knowledge with new vocabulary. After the teacher has introduced a vocabulary word, such as *tranquil*, in both definitional and contextual situations, the students would be asked to make a word card and give their personal definitions and contextual meanings for the word. Below is a student's card for the word *tranquil*. Students can use this strategy as a means for developing independence in vocabulary learning by applying the technique to words that are learned through their own reading and listening experiences.

Tranquil

Definitions   *Personal examples*
quiet   forest at summer camp
calm   Aunt Alice
                          Lake Westwood

PREDICT-O-GRAM

The Predict-o-Gram (Blanchowicz, 1986) combines vocabulary development with story structure awareness. Students are encouraged to make predictions about how the author will use vocabulary to tell about the setting, characters, the problem or goal, the actions, resolution, or feeling of a character in a story. Given the following vocabulary for a narrative story like *Sleeping Beauty*, students would be asked to classify the words according to how they predict the author might use them in the story.

Students can learn to use this strategy independently when they encounter vocabulary lists by predicting how the words relate to the elements of story structure.

2. Developing Elaborated Word Knowledge

Engaging students in manipulating words in varied and rich ways produces a deeper understanding of the words and more flexibility in using the words (Beck, McKeown, & Omanson, 1984). Enhancing the richness of word knowledge can be accomplished by providing multiple contexts for new vocabulary words. This promotes expanded word knowledge and a broader understanding of the meanings of words. Both the *context-repetition procedure* and the *definition/example word cards* provide multiple contexts for the new vocabulary words in addition to encouraging students to access prior knowledge. The following are additional examples of instructional procedures and

---

Sleeping Beauty

princess
spinning
dead
evil
awaken
forest
lies
castle
happily

Sleeping Beauty

The setting
forest
castle

The characters
princess
evil

The goal or problem
dead
awaken

The actions
lies
spinning

The resolution
happily

---

strategies that are appropriate for enhancing the elaborated word knowledge.

SEMANTIC CATEGORIES

This procedure involves introducing new vocabulary words through the use of semantic categories. New words are introduced in a word list that deals with a specific semantic category. Gipe (1980) suggests that each word list contain one unknown word and three familiar words. Students are directed to study the list and add words to the list from their personal background. For example, the category heading of *Bad People* might be used to introduce the new word *barbarian*. Three familiar words, such as *mean*, *cruel*, and *robber*, would be used in the word list to provide clues to the meaning of the unfamiliar word. Below is an example of student words added to the category of *Bad People*:

Bad People

mean
robber
barbarian
wicked

cruel

thief

Using categories of words that are semantically related helps students build relationships among words and results in a richer understanding of each word's meaning (Carr & Wixson, 1986). In addition, this activity also encourages students to access their prior knowledge by relating the words in the word list to words they know that fit the category.

WORD CONNECTIONS

Given a word list from a basal story or content textbook, Blanchowicz (1986) suggests that students use the word connection procedure to broaden word meaning knowledge. Students pick any two words from the instructional word list and tell how they might be related. For example, the instructional word list for the story *Family Life in an African Bush Station* might look like the following:

Family Life in an African Bush Station

thicket	bush
pampas	antelope

A student might choose to connect *pampas* and *thicket* because a thicket can be made up of clumps of pampas grass. Another student might connect *antelope* and *thicket* because an antelope might hide in a thicket. Word connection is a simple form of classification. It is very important to recognize that it is *through the discussion about why or how the words relate to each other* that vocabulary knowledge is enriched in the word-connection activity. Students can be encouraged to develop independence in the use of this strategy by having them make connections between and among the vocabulary words that are presented for basal stories and at the beginning or end of content units. Students should be taught to preview word lists independently prior to reading, and to make as many word connections as possible, in order to activate prior knowledge and strengthen their personal framework for comprehending the text.

VOCABULARY COMPARE/ CONTRAST PROCEDURE

One way to engage students in discovering vocabulary relationships is to pose questions that will pique their curiosity (Johnson & Pearson, 1984). Beck, McKeown & Omanson (1984) suggest that students compare and contrast the features of two new words. Students could be asked, for example, "Would you *berate* someone who *inspired* you?" or "Could a *philanthropist* be a *miser?*" The students then discuss how the words are associated with each other.

3. Providing for Active Student Involvement

The success of vocabulary instruction is greatly affected by the degree of active student involvement in the learning process (Mezynski,

1983). Simply attempting to memorize definitions that match specific words does not produce lasting ownership of words.

SEMANTIC FEATURE ANALYSIS—VOCABULARY GRID

Semantic feature analysis is an activity that focuses upon the vocabulary and concepts needed for comprehension (Anders & Bos, 1986; Johnson & Pearson, 1984). With very young children we use the term *vocabulary grid* instead of the more sophistocated term *semantic feature analysis*. The vocabulary grid activity helps students learn new vocabulary that represents the ideas being presented in a story or content textbook. The most significant feature of a vocabulary grid is that it enables students to learn the relationships between and among the vocabulary and the major ideas presented in the text.

The first step in developing a vocabulary grid involves reading the text and listing, in phrase or single words, the vocabulary that represents significant ideas in the text. Next, the vocabulary should be organized into a relationship chart, the grid (see the example below). This grid becomes the instructional tool. The grid can be duplicated for student use, or it can be put on an overhead. This activity is most effective when presented through teacher modeling. The teacher would introduce the vocabulary and concepts on a word grid and would lead a discussion concerning the relationships that exist among the words and the concepts.

The key to success in the use of the vocabulary grid is the student involvement during the discussion. To encourage and facilitate student involvement, ask students to explain why and how the words on the grid are or are not related. A vocabulary grid is most effectively used to introduce vocabulary and concepts prior to the reading of the story or text. After completing the grid, students should read to confirm the accuracy of their predictions concerning the relationships among the words and concepts represented on the grid. In addition to the high level of student involvement that the vocabulary grid encourages, this activity allows students to activate prior knowledge and to think

Vocabulary Grid

DESERTS						
	low rainfall	sand	hot	eastern hemisphere	nomadic life	irrigation
Gobi	✓	✓	✓	✓		
Sahara	✓	✓	✓		✓	
Mohavi	✓	✓	✓			
Sonora	✓	✓	✓			
Negev	✓	✓	✓	✓		✓

about the relationships between and among their prior knowledge and the new vocabulary (Anders & Bos, 1986).

VOCABULARY KNOWLEDGE RATING

To encourgage students to analyze what they know about new vocabulary, Blanchowicz (1986) suggests the procedure of vocabulary knowledge rating. Before the reading of a story or content textbook unit, students are presented with a list of vocabulary. The teacher has them analyze what they know about each word and indicates on the chart their level of word knowledge. This procedure is most effective when used as a springboard to class discussion. The teacher can encourage students to share what they know or think they know about the words on the list.

4. Developing Independence in Vocabulary Learning

Vocabulary instruction should stress the importance of students' being able to figure out new words on their own. Students should

DESERT LIFE			
How much do I know about these words?	Can define	Have seen/heard	?
desert	✓		
nomad		✓	
wanderer	✓		
settler	✓		
Gobi			✓

have a repertoire of strategies that allow them to gain control of the vocabulary-acquisition process. According to Schwartz and Raphael (1985) one of the major comprehension activities required when reading content textbooks is learning the meaning of new words. Therefore, students need to own strategies they can use to expand their vocabularies and master unfamiliar concepts.

WORD MAPS

A word map, as developed by Schwartz and Raphael (1985), is a visual representation of a definition. Categories of relationships are used in word maps: (1) the general class to which the concept belongs, (2) the primary properties of the concept and those that distinguish it from other members of the class, and (3) examples and nonexamples of the concept. These categories are translated into questions to guide elementary students in their search for a word's meaning: (1) What is it? (2) What is it like? (3) What are some examples, and what are some nonexamples? This procedure should be introduced through

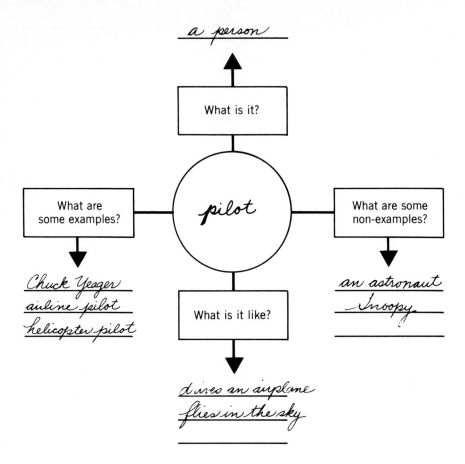

teacher modeling. Gradually students are led to assume responsibility for developing word maps independently.

In the center of the map, students write a new vocabulary word, such as *pilot*, as seen in the example above. (Nouns are most appropriate for this activity, but action words and other parts of speech can also be used effectively.) Next they write a general word that answers the question "What is it?" The answer to "What is it like?" specifies those features that distinguish a pilot from other types of driver. The answer to "What are some examples?" requires that the student develop examples of the word being defined, while the answer to "What are some nonexamples?" tells what the word does not describe or define.

Using this procedure, students internalize the concept of definition as they answer the questions "What is it?" "What is it like?" "What are some examples?" and "What are some nonexamples?" Internalization of the concept of definition is necessary for students to develop independence in acquiring new vocabulary through reading. Students can be encouraged to develop independent use of this strategy by providing them with the basic frame provided in the illustration and encouraging them to use word maps for new vocabulary words that they would like to learn and remember.

FIVE STEPS TO VOCABULARY INDEPENDENCE

Blanchowicz (1986) has suggested five practical steps that readers can be taught in order to promote independence in vocabulary growth. Given a vocabulary list from a story or content textbook, the student can use the following steps:

1. Trigger background knowledge. Ask myself, "What do I already know about these words?"
2. Preview the story (selection) for clues as to what the words might mean.
3. Read the text.
4. Refine and reformulate predicted meanings of the vocabulary based on information gained from reading the text.
5. To make a new word mine, I must read it and use it. Use new vocabulary in writing and be alert to the word in future reading.

5. Valuing Word Knowledge

Ideally, all the preceding instructional procedures and strategies would be in keeping with the guideline and goal of helping students learn to value word knowledge. We want students to value word knowledge and to carry their vocabulary learning beyond the classroom.

WORD WIZARD

Beck and McKeown (1983) suggest an activity that is specifically designed to encourage students to expand their vocabulary activities beyond the classroom. To became a Word Wizard the student identifies new and interesting vocabulary words that he or she has seen, heard, or used outside the class. Students earn points for bringing in words to share with the class. The words that are shared with the class can be recorded in the students' individual vocabulary notebooks. Each word added to the notebook is worth a specified number of points. As points are accumulated students move to successive levels: Word Worker, Word Whirlwind, Word Wizard, and Wonderful Word Wizard. For example, if each word is worth 5 points, a total of 30 points (six words) would earn the student a certificate as a Word Worker, 60 points might be required for Word Whirlwind, 90 points for Word Wizard, and 125 points for Wonderful Word Wizard. The purpose of this activity is to provide extrinsic motivation for students to extend their vocabulary learning beyond the confines of the classroom.

CONGRATULATIONS!

This award of special recognition is presented to ___*Scott*___ in recognition of ___*his*___ vocabulary knowledge. ___*He*___ is hereby appointed **Wonderful Word Wizard!**

Wonderful
WORD WIZARD*!*

ASSESSING TEXT MATERIALS
FOR VOCABULARY
INSTRUCTION

Effective vocabulary instruction involves making assessments with
regard to the text materials that students will use in learning situations. Instruction then focuses upon making adjustments to close the
gap between the student's vocabulary knowledge and the vocabulary
used in the text (Coley & Gambrell, 1977).

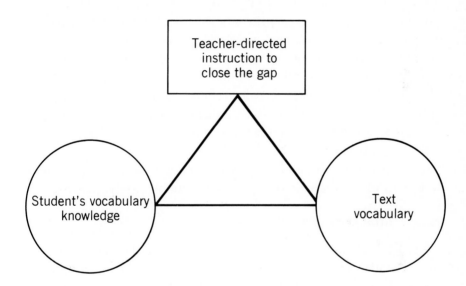

In order to provide effective instruction the teacher must evaluate
the vocabulary of the text material to be used for instruction and
provide appropriate vocabulary instruction when necessary. The number of text factors that might be assessed with respect to the reading
vocabulary is almost limitless. One reason for the enormous number
of factors is that texts are so diverse. With the categorizing of instructional texts by type (such as basal readers, language experience stories,
trade books, etc.), some common characteristics do emerge for consideration. Each type of text has certain strengths with respect to
treatment of reading vocabulary. These strengths should be used to

help students develop their reading vocabulary. Likewise, each type of text has limitations for which teachers must compensate.

The chart (p. 87) lists *general* characteristics with respect to vocabulary instruction typical of a variety of text materials used for reading instruction. Specific text materials used for instruction should be carefully examined because there are great variations among the characteristics of certain types of text material.

The designation "strong" on the chart suggests that the text material is well exemplified, in general, by that characteristic. For instance, the designation "strong" in the experiential background category for language experience stories indicates that there is a close match between the student's vocabulary and the vocabulary of the experience story. For the category of word repetitions, the language experience approach is rated "weak." This should alert the teacher to the need to provide additional instruction with regard to word repetitions. On the chart, "variable" indicates that the text material is not stable for that characteristic. For example, in the category of experiential background, basal readers receive a designation of "variable." Sometimes the student's background of experiences may mesh well with the story; however, this would not always be the case.

Experiential Background

Special attention should be given to assessing the match between the student's background of experiences and the story or information presented in the text used for instruction. Experiential background can be developed through a variety of experiences. For instance, a class getting ready to study African wildlife might take a trip to the zoo to see the animals about which they are going to read. Experiential background can also be developed through vicarious experiences provided by slides, movies, and other motivational media. By providing experiential background the teacher makes it more likely that the new words that students encounter in text will be recognized and comprehended.

Repetitions

The student's retention of new words is affected by the number

General Text Characteristics

TEXT TYPE	Matches student's experiential background	Provides systematic word repetitions	Not complicated with high concept load/density
Basal Reader	Variable	Strong	Strong
Language Experience Story	Strong	Weak	Strong
Content Textbook	Variable	Weak	Weak
Trade Book	Variable	Weak	Variable

of meaningful encounters with the new word. Basal readers are characterized by the use of a controlled vocabulary. Controlled vocabulary means that the number and types of new words are systematically introduced and repeated. The repetitions are carefully planned and sequenced so that students encounter a new word a number of times throughout the text. This repetition is done to help reinforce the learning of the new words. Language experience materials, content textbooks, and trade or library books do not usually have controlled vocabularies. That is, there is no systematic attempt to introduce new words at a given rate, nor are repetitions systematically provided for new words. Teachers can compensate for the lack of repetition in language experience materials, textbooks, and trade books through instructional activities that provide opportunities for meaninful repetitions of new words.

Concept Load and Concept Density

The ultimate aim of text materials is to convey concepts to the reader. Vocabulary embodies these concepts, sometimes in the form of a single word like *osmosis*, at other times by means of many words to explain a unified idea, for example, "passage of a liquid through a permeable or semipermeable membrane." Basal readers designed for the teaching of beginning reading are not typically complicated by concepts foreign to the young child. On the other hand, textbooks and trade books often contain concepts that are not familiar to the reader.

The concept load presented in a text may range from high to low. When a text has a number of unfamiliar concepts, it has a high concept load, which may make comprehension difficult for the reader. Concept density refers to the concentration of concepts within a given unit of text. Many new words and concepts may be introduced within the first couple of pages of a text; the concept density in such a case is high. It may be difficult for the student to comprehend fully because of the concept density.

CHAPTER SUMMARY

Vocabulary knowledge is an integral component of reading comprehension. This chapter has focused upon instructional procedures and strategies for enhancing vocabulary knowledge. The five guidelines for vocabulary instruction emphasized relating new vocabulary to students' background knowledge, developing elaborated word knowledge, providing for active involvement in learning, developing independence, and valuing word knowledge. Instructional strategies that exemplify the five guidelines were discussed. Finally, considerations were presented for assessing text materials for vocabulary instruction.

REFERENCES

Anders, P. L., & Bos, C. S. (1986). Semantic feature analysis: An interactive strategy for vocabulary development and text comprehension. *Journal of Reading, 29,* 610–616.

Beck, I. L., & McKeown, M. G. (1983). Learning words well—A Program to enhance vocabulary and comprehension. *The Reading Teacher, 36,* 622–625.

Beck, I. L., McKeown, M. G., & Omanson, R. C. (1984, April). *The fertility of some types of vocabulary instruction.* Paper presented at the meeting of the American Educational Research Association, New Orleans, La.

Beck, I. L., Perfetti, C. A., & McKeown, M. G. (1982). Effects of long-term vocabulary instruction on lexical access and reading comprehension. *Journal of Educational Psychology, 74,* 506–521.

Blanchowicz, C. L. (1986). Making connections: Alternatives to the vocabulary note-book. *Journal of Reading, 29,* 643–649.

Carr, E., & Wixson, K. K. (1986). Guidelines for evaluating vocabulary instruction. *Journal of Reading, 29,* 588–595.

Coley, J. D., & Gambrell, L. B. (1977). *Programmed reading vocabulary for teachers.* Columbus, Ohio: Merrill.

Craik, F., & Lockhart, R. (1972). Levels of processing: A framework for memory research. *Journal of Verbal Learning and Verbal Behavior, 11,* 671–684.

Dale, E., & O'Rourke, J. (1971). *Techniques of teaching vocabulary.* Palo Alto, Calif.: Field Educational Publications.

Eeds, M., & Cockrum, W. A. (1985). Teaching word meanings by expanding schemata vs. dictionary work vs. reading in context. *Journal of Reading, 28,* 492–497.

Gipe, J. P. (1980). Use of relevant context helps kids learn new word meanings. *The Reading Teacher, 33,* 398–402.

Graves, M. F. (in press). The roles of instruction in fostering vocabulary development. In M. G. McKeown & M. E. Curtis (Eds.), *The nature of vocabulary acquisition.* Hillsdale, N.J.: Erlbaum.

Graves, M. F., & Prinn, M. C. (1986). Costs and benefits of various methods of teaching vocabulary. *Journal of Reading, 29,* 596–602.

Jenkins, J. R., Stein, M. L., & Wysocki, K. (1984). Learning vocabulary through reading. *American Educational Research Journal, 21,* 767–787.

Johnson, D. D., & Pearson, P. D. (1984). *Teaching reading vocabulary.* New York: Holt, Rinehart and Winston.

Mezynski, K. (1983). Issues concerning the acquisition of knowledge: Effects of vo-cabulary training on reading comprehension. *Review of Educational Research, 53,* 253–279.

Nagy, W. E., Herman, P. A., & Anderson, R. C. (1985). Learning words from context. *Reading Research Quarterly, 20,* 233–253.

Nelson-Herber, J. (1986). Expanding and refining vocabulary in content areas. *Journal of Reading, 29,* 626–633.

Ruddell, R. B. (1986). Vocabulary learning: A process model and criteria for evaluating instructional strategies. *Journal of Reading, 29,* 581–587.

Schwartz, R. M., & Raphael, T. E. (1985). Concept of definition: A key to improving students' vocabulary. *The Reading Teacher, 39,* 198–205.

Stahl, S. A. (1983). Differential word knowledge and reading comprehension. *Journal of Reading Behavior, 15,* 33–47.

Stahl, S. A. (1986). Three principles of effective vocabulary instruction. *Journal of Reading, 29,* 662–668.

Stahl, S. A., & Fairbanks, M. M. (1986). The effects of vocabulary instruction: A model-based meta-analysis. *Review of Educational Research, 56,* 72–110.

Questioning for Comprehension of Text 7

Asking the right question at the right time can aid in the comprehension process; asking the wrong question at the wrong time can deter the comprehension process. This chapter will examine the various aspects of questioning and timing as they relate to comprehension. Teachers have many decisions to make about questioning. Questions following reading can be used as an aid to or an assessment of comprehension. In this chapter we want to emphasize the use of questions as an aid to comprehension. Teachers can ask questions to stimulate their students' thinking about what has been read. The responses of one student can trigger the thinking of other students. It has long been recognized that students learn from one another just as they learn from their teachers.

We will start with a vignette.

THE ADLER VIGNETTE

Mr. Adler was viewed by his peers as an experienced and effective teacher. While he felt good about most of his reading instruction, he was very concerned about some of his students' responses to reading comprehension activities. He taught a mixed group of fifth graders in an inner-city school. He understood the need for him to ask good

(continued)

---

questions. He also knew of his students' need for prior knowledge if they were to understand text information. But despite his best efforts, many of his students (good and poor readers alike) did not seem to gain as much understanding from text as he would have liked. He finally decided that the questions he was asking were too difficult for his students. He consulted with his teaching peers, his principal, and his reading supervisor; they all seemed to agree that he might try asking easier questions. Now the problem was, what makes a question easier? He finally decided that it would be easier to answer questions that were personal, that is, questions that could be answered without the teacher's approval of the answer. First, he decided how he might best frame "personal questions." He thought it might be best to start all of his questioning with requests for an opinion. So he decided to start with personal question stems such as:

- "What do you think . . . ?"
- "What interested you about . . . ?"
- "How would you have handled . . . ?"

After one week with the use of these types of starter question he was delighted at the students' responses. While he did not personally agree with each response, he quickly saw that various students were using their different background experiences to develop their "personal" answers to his personal questions. He shared his success with others, and they were also excited about the notion of asking personal questions to start the reading lesson. Many of his peers decided to try it and were equally pleased with the results.

While there may have been many other solutions to Mr. Adler's concern about his students' reading comprehension, we believe this was a good "first" decision. He seemed to have found a temporary solution to the problems that his students were experiencing. He wanted to evaluate this strategy over a number of lessons to determine whether the students' comprehension continued to improve.

We'll be returning to this vignette to illustrate some teacher decision options during the reading comprehension lesson. We'll refer to it as the "Adler Vignette," so you might want to mark the pages of this vignette for easy referral.

QUESTION TYPES

There are many ways to classify questions. Some authorities have made very complex classification systems that are usually referred to as "taxonomies." A word of caution must be extended concerning the use of taxonomies. That caution is concerned with the hierarchical nature implied or directly stated by the developer of the taxonomy. The very notion of a hierarchy of question types leads one to believe that the lower-level types of questions must be mastered before going to the higher-level question types. Indeed, many educators believe that the higher-level questions should be used with gifted students while the lower-level questions should be used with remedial readers. This notion of question levels applied to the way students can think about what they have read is offensive. The fact that by the age of six most children can watch television programs, understand humor in the programs, make predictions about what might be going to happen next, understand implied meanings, and search for resolutions of the program's problems would argue that almost all children can handle many thought processes from simple to complex. Why, then, should educators want to limit the types of questions asked in reading lessons?

In the Adler Vignette a decision was made to start asking students personal questions. These questions would rank rather high on most taxonomies. But they are easy for students to respond to because the student is the only one who has the correct answer.

We have had considerable experience with asking personal questions at the start of reading comprehension lessons and have found that:

- students respond well to them
- students enjoy them
- students answer other types of questions better when they are started with personal questions.

We will argue for the case that teachers should start all reading comprehension lessons with personal questions. It seems logical that the starter questions should be answerable by every student. That creates a situation that allows for immediate success and could change the entire feeling that students might have concerning the reading comprehension lesson. For that reason alone, starting with personal questions carries considerable merit. Of course, there are other merits to personal questions. They stimulate thinking about the text that has been read. They provide teachers, by way of students' responses, with evidence about the understandings that the students have had about the text that has been read. There are no penalties because of wrong answers at the outset of the lesson. Students need not be embarrassed about their answer: It's personal. If the student says, "I'm not sure" or "I don't know," that is acceptable because the starter question was personal.

Even if the text contains material that is expository, as in science or social studies, teachers can easily start with personal questions. Starter questions can be followed with those that ask for justification for the answer or with those that ask for the location in the text of information that suggested the first answer. This is not meant to challenge the student's answer, but to suggest to the student that he or she has a responsibility for his or her answers.

TYPES OF QUESTIONS

We use the term "types of questions" instead of "levels of questions" for the reasons given above. If the reader finds other texts using "levels of questions," the subject is the same as ours—without, it is hoped, any spurious hierarchies of difficulty implied.

For the purposes of discussion about question types this text will be using the following terms:

- literal questions
- interpretive questions
- critical questions
- creative questions

Most questions that teachers ask fit nicely into these types of categories.

Literal questions. Literal questions ask for responses that are directly stated in the text. Their primary use is to assess whether students comprehended the information in the passage. Using the Adler Vignette, they might include:

- Who was the teacher in this story?
- To whom did he go for advice?
- What type of questions did he decide to use?

Literal questions ask for facts, sequences, and details. Are they important? Of course they are. Do they justify the use by teachers for 80 to 90 percent of the questions asked of students? We'd say a strong "NO!" While the literal understanding of text is necessary for many reading activities, such as following the steps in a science experiment or following a recipe for making cookies, many of the questions asked of students are not important. Why, then, are they used so often? It is because they are easy to form and evaluate. The answers are either right or wrong. It takes little effort to use these types of questions, so teachers use them often.

If the teacher wants to know whether students understand the literal meanings from text, it is best that the students can refer to the text, if needed. This reduces the load on memory and maintains the ability to demonstrate literal comprehension of the text. In most cases the memory of literal information is unimportant; when it is important, the text should not be available, of course. For example, it might not be very important to remember the name of the teacher in the Adler Vignette. On the other hand, it might be very important to know what chemicals should never be mixed or to remember how to act in a firedrill. Teachers need to make clear and important decisions about the use of text when asking literal questions.

Most teachers have gone through schooling that requires the memorization of unimportant facts. As they have been taught, so they teach. But we ask you to consider the reason for asking students to remember unimportant facts from text. One can readily evaluate whether or not a student understands the facts of a story without resorting to questions that require memory. For example, is there any importance in remembering the name of the teacher in the Adler

Vignette? Can one perfectly understand the Adler Vignette without remembering his name? Of course one can.

Teachers should use literal questions with much consideration about the purpose of those questions. Asking them because they are easy to form and easy to evalaute should not be the determining factor. The determining factor must be related to the importance of the information that the questions seek.

Interpretive questions. Interpretive questions ask for students to respond to implied meanings in a text. The answers to these questions are not found directly in the text, but there is information in the text that suggests appropriate responses. Using the Adler Vignette once again, we'll form some interpretive questions.

- Was Mr. Adler a beginning teacher?
- Who were Mr. Adler's peers?
- With whom did Mr. Adler not share his successes?

None of the questions' answers is directly stated in the text. But the text offers information that allows readers to answer these questions. For the first one, the text did say that he was an experienced teacher. One would therefore infer that he was not a beginning teacher, although the text did not state how long he had been teaching. To answer the second question the reader needs to use prior knowledge about those who are a teacher's peers: His peers are not his students, his principal, or his reading supervisor; they must be his fellow teachers. For the third answer the reader needs to remember that Mr. Adler shared his success with his peers. The text did not say that he did not share his success with his principal and his reading supervisor, and we cannot be sure that he neglected to share his discovery with them; however, we can *infer* that he shared his success only with his peers.

Interpretive questions are more difficult to form, and their answers are more difficult to evaluate. For example, the readers might argue that, in response to the third question, his principal should not be excluded. It would only be logical for Mr. Adler to share his successes with his principal. Interpretive questions generate a more interesting thought process than literal answers require. Students enjoy thinking about the answers. Since, at times, there is more than one correct or logical answer, there is more room for a successful answer.

Teachers need to prepare themselves for appropriate responses to the answers of their students. since the correctness of any answer is based on several factors, teachers need to gain an understanding of how a given response had been developed. For example, to an elementary school student a beginning teacher might seem to be quite experienced. Such a student might argue that Mr. Adler might have been a Boy Scout leader or a Sunday school teacher and had a lot of teaching experience. A possible response to this is "You might be correct. Many teachers have had teaching experiences before they start in a classroom. But we are going to answer our questions based on information from the text. Based on information from the text, what would your answer be?"

Critical questions. Critical questions call upon readers to examine the text to evaluate a decision or an event. Critical questions also require readers to use their prior knowledge when making these evaluations and critiques. They are useful in helping readers challenge the ideas in text; they help students to understand that they often have valid and important ideas about what they have read. When critical questions are not used, the readers may get the idea that what they have read is right just because it appears in print.

Using the Adler Vignette, we'll frame a couple of critical questions for examination:

- Do you think Mr. Adler was correct in his decision to make his questions easier?
- Do you think that one week was long enough for Mr. Adler to decide he had been successful?
- Why would Mr. Adler's peers decide to try what he had reported as successful?

Once again, the answers to some of these questions could take several forms, and each form could be correct. The students' prior knowledge in a given area might lead to a response that others had not thought of. This is not to say that all critical questions have more than one correct answer. Indeed, some would have only one acceptable answer because of the nature of the text from which they were formed.

Critical questions are often followed by other questions that relate to the original question. For example, if a student's response to the first question above was "yes," the teacher might request a reason or might ask what information in the text justified this answer. With these types of questions the follow-up questions might be more important than the original questions.

Creative questions. Creative questions call for the students to go beyond the text and to use their imaginations. They call for divergent thought processes.

Using the Adler Vignette, here are some we formed as examples:

- How else might Mr. Adler have changed his questions to make them easier?
- What do you think would have happened if Mr. Adler had not consulted his peers, his principal, and his reading supervisor?
- What should Mr. Adler have done if, after one week, the students continued to have difficulty answering his questions?

These questions ask for students' opinions. They clearly have no correct answers. As with critical questions, creative questions often require follow-up questions that ask students for justification for their answers. For example, if an answer to the third creative question was "Try them for another week," the teacher might ask, "Why do you think two weeks would get better results?" Again, this is not meant as a challenge to the student's answer, but to stimulate students' thinking or to obtain more information about the students' thought processes.

Creative questions are enjoyable for students to answer because they create a discussion atmosphere. These discussions can get quite lively, especially when students have strong opinions about their answers. At times a student might give an answer for which there is no apparent justification. Sometimes their answers are just silly. To avoid these two situations teachers need to establish an atmosphere of serious intent. They need to communicate that it is important that students present their best thinking when responding to creative questions. To do less is a waste of everyone's time.

While creative questions are stimulating to the thinking process, they will not be found on standardized tests. Standardized tests require questions for which there is only one correct response. Teachers need to be aware that these types of questions, however, can improve test scores because they can stimulate students' thought processes. Those stimulated thought processes can indeed improve standardized test performance.

WAIT TIME

Another aspect of questioning has to do with "wait time." Wait time was described by Rowe (1973) as the amount of time a teacher waits between asking a question and calling for an answer. She found that teachers allowed very little wait time—less than one second in most cases. For all of the question types mentioned above, however, students need time to think about an appropriate response. Most teachers have experienced the situation in which some students start to wave their hands before the question has even been completed. Often, when called upon, these students do not have any idea how to respond. Rowe contends, and we agree, that students should be instructed to wait until asked for a response; a time of three or more seconds is recommended. We have noticed that allowing students wait time increases the accuracy of their responses. Once understood by students, it can also reduce the hand waving before the questions are asked.

Lyman, a teacher center coordinator in Howard County, Maryland, has developed a good system for helping students respond with wait time (Lyman, Lopez, & Mindus, 1977). He suggests that teachers use a visual system to let students know when to respond; a visual cue can be used to suggest to students that it is time to think, not respond. One visual cue that he suggests is the use of a picture cube. On one side the word "Read" is written; on the next side is the word "Think." Students are instructed that the word "Think" means to wait and not respond. More of using this cube will be discussed in the next section, but it works well to help students understand the need to think before responding. Other visual cues, such as poster cards or chalkboard instructions, could be used.

Another aspect of wait time that Rowe described relates to the amount of time teachers wait for student responses to questions. She found that teachers usually do not wait any length of time at all. In fact, some teachers do not even let students finish their response; they interrupt before the student response has been completed. By waiting just a few seconds Rowe found that students will continue with their response, making a more complete response to the question. She also noticed that other students will respond to the first student, creating a discussion atmosphere. While some teachers might feel a bit uncomfortable using this second type of wait time, a few sessions of practice will make them feel at ease. Perhaps they have become so accustomed to the classroom flow of quick responses that the silence bothers them. They might feel a lack of control. If this is the case, we suggest that teachers try this type of wait time occasionally for short periods of time. They will grow more comfortable with wait time after using it awhile.

THINK–PAIR–SHARE

Mention was made of the advantage of supplying students with visual cues for the behavior desired during questioning. Lyman suggests the use of a picture cube when working in small groups. The cube has six sides so that teachers can place six different behaviors on the cube. For starters we suggest the behaviors "Read," "Write," "Listen," "Think," "Pair," and "Share." A brief description of how these commands work might help those unfamiliar with the use of visual cueing.

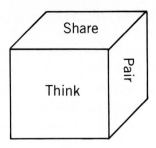

"Read." Here the teacher obviously wants all the children involved in the group to be reading. It may be assigned text or it may be student selected; the choice is up to the teacher.

"Write." After the reading is completed, a writing activity might be expected. The "Write" cue tells the students that reading time is over and it is time to complete the writing activity.

"Listen." If the teacher decides to give some directions or ask some questions, the "Listen" cue is displayed. This tells the students to listen because the teacher is going to provide some important information. This is not the time for talking or for raising hands to answer questions.

"Think." While waiting for the students to think about their answer(s), the teacher displays the "Think" cue. This tells students to think about an answer during the "Think" time.

"Pair." At times a teacher might want students to discuss their answers in pairs before sharing them with the group. The "Pair" cue instructs the students to do just that. There are some advantages for the pairing activity. Answers are tested on a peer who may or may not agree. The two students can discuss the pros and cons of a given answer. If the answer needs some refining, it can be done in the pair mode. The two students might combine their personal answers to make one answer that is better than either of the personal ones. A buzzing sound is created in the classroom by "Pairs," but it is a good sound, not a disruptive one. The teacher can move around and listen to various pairs. If some students get off-task, the teacher can help them to get back on-task. The group response rate becomes very high,

since instead of one student attempting to answer the questions, all students are attempting it.

"Share." Now the students can raise their hands to be called upon for their answers. They have listened to the question, thought about their answer, tested their response with a peer, and are ready to share their response with the group and the teacher. We have noticed that students' responses tend to be very well developed when using this cueing system.

Lyman suggests that the cueing sequence of "Think–Pair–Share" results in better reading comprehension. The three cues should be used in the sequence suggested to obtain the best results.

Obviously, teachers can use any cues and any sequences that make the best sense to them and their students. Trying reading comprehension instruction with some type of visual cueing to assist students in understanding the expected behavior makes good sense to us. It is efficient, quick, and a quiet way to operate in a classroom. Students in other parts of the classroom who are studying independently are not bothered by a lot of teacher's verbal requests. It lets students know what behavior is expected, something that many students must make a guess at because there is no announced expectation. It increases student responses and improves on-task behavior. We have used the visual cueing idea with remedial readers of all ages in our reading clinic and have been very pleased with the resulting student behaviors.

STORY GRAMMAR QUESTIONS

Questions that tap cognitive skills (literal, interpretive, critical, and creative) serve a useful function for teachers. They let teachers know how students are thinking about the ideas in the text. They also help to provide students with different ways to think about the material that has been read. Story grammar questions serve a different function. They help students understand the structure of the story in the text.

Most stories carry a series of similar structures. Those structures include:

- establishment of a setting
- something that started a series of events (initiating activity)
- how characters reacted (reaction)
- what the characters did about their situation (action)
- the result of the action (consequences)

Sadow (1982) suggests that teachers develop questions for each of the above-mentioned structures so that students develop an understanding of the sequence of events common to most stories. Using the Adler Vignette, we will form some of these questions to illustrate story grammar.

Establishing setting—	What was Mr. Adler's occupation?
	Where did he teach?
	What grade level did he teach?
Initiating activity—	What was Mr. Adler's concern?
• Reaction—	How did Mr. Adler decide to make a change in his questioning?
• Action—	What did Mr. Adler do to correct his concern?
• Consequences—	How did his students respond?
	How did his peers respond?

Sadow claimed that story grammar questions help students internalize text information beyond the sentence and paragraph level of importance. While such awareness might or might not have an effect upon the students' cognitive knowledge about story information, it does seem logical that they might be better able to anticipate how stories are developed. As they read stories in the future they can apply what they have learned through lessons that used story grammar questions.

We'd suggest that teachers try story grammar questions on a periodic basis and evaluate their students' responses to them. Story grammar questions change the questioning routine and add a potentially powerful way for students to gain insight to story structure.

STUDENT-DEVELOPED
QUESTIONS

The teachers need not be the only developer of questions. Students can develop them also. Teachers can ask students to read a selection from text and form questions for their peers. Think for a minute about what is involved with student-developed questions:

- They need to understand the story.
- They need to think about what was important.
- They need to determine what would be an appropriate answer.
- They need to think about how to respond to any answer.

We have observed that students enjoy forming questions for their peers and their peers seem to enjoy answering them. The major activity of understanding the story focuses upon the students instead of the teacher. By taking this responsibility, the students become actively involved in thinking about what is and is not important in the story they have read.

Students can also form questions for the teacher to answer. This provides a major switch in roles. And students really enjoy changing roles with the teacher. Teachers might want to set some procedures for this activity. For example, the teacher might decide that today all student questions will be critical or creative ones. This helps to keep the students moving toward desired educational objectives.

Reading comprehension can also be evaluated from the types of questions students develop. If they are not important and are not related to story events, the teacher has some information for further teacher-directed activities. On the other hand, if they are relevant and appropriate to the story content, the teacher can assume that reading comprehension has been achieved.

QUESTION-ANSWERING
STRATEGIES

Teaching question–answer relationships (QARs) can help students become more successful at answering questions about what they have read. Questions can be categorized according to the source of the information required for the answer. Students can be taught to analyze questions to determine the source of information necessary for determining the correct answer. There are three specific strategies that students can use to find the information they need to answer questions (Raphael, 1982): Right There, Think and Search, and On My Own.

WHERE WILL I FIND THE ANSWER?

Right There

The answer will be in the story. It will be easy to find. The words in the question and the words needed for the answer will be *right there* in the same sentence.

Think and Search

The answer will be in the story but a little harder to find. I would never find the very same words in the question and the words for the answer in the same sentence. I will have to *think and search* for the answer.

On My Own

The words for the answer will not be in the story. I will have to find information to answer the question in my own head.

Raphael and Pearson (1982) found that students who had been taught the three QARs were more successful in answering questions than were students who had not received the strategy instruction. They suggest some tips for successfully teaching students to use QARs:

1. Select a passage and appropriate questions. Model the process of determining the source of information for answering the three types of questions.
2. Provide practice passages and questions for students to decide on the appropriate strategy for determining the answer. Progress from shorter to longer texts.
3. Give immediate feedback with respect to the student's ability to determine the correct QAR and his or her ability to provide an adequate response to the question.
4. Build independence by guiding students from working in a group to independent application of the strategies.
5. Be accepting of diverse responses. Students should be en-

couraged to justify their responses on the basis of the text and their own prior knowledge. The teacher should explain *why* an answer is appropriate with respect to both accuracy and strategy and recognize that more than one answer may be appropriate.

A game was developed by Raphael and Wonnacott (1981) to encourage discussion of the concepts underlying question–answer relationships. The game involves having some students act as lawyers. The lawyers are responsible for stating the type of QAR represented by a question and defending their reasoning by explaining the source of the most appropriate response. The remaining students may raise objections and present a defense if an alternative QAR or response is determined. This activity involves students in verbalizing their thought processes and provides an opportunity for clarification of the process and any misunderstanding that might occur.

CHAPTER SUMMARY

Questioning is a common practice in most classrooms. By understanding some of the options available during questioning, teachers can prevent lessons from becoming repetitious. Teachers must decide whether they will use questions to stimulate student thinking about what has been read or whether they want to use questions to assess student comprehension.

The remainder of this book will examine some of the other factors that affect reading comprehension instruction.

REFERENCES

Lyman, F., Lopez, C., & Mindus, A. (1977). *Elementary Language Arts Guide*. Clarksville, Md.: Howard County Board of Education.

Raphael, T. E. (1982). Question-answering strategies for children. *The Reading Teacher, 36,* 186–190.

Raphael, T. E., & Pearson, P. D. (1982). The effect of metacognitive awareness training on children's question answering behavior. *Technical Report #238.* Urbana, Ill.: Center for the Study of Reading, University of Illinois.

Raphael, R. E., & Wonnacott, C. A. (1981). The effect of metacognitive training on question-answering behavior: Implementation in a fourth grade developmental reading program. Paper presented at the National Reading Conference, Dallas, Tex.

Rowe, M. B. (1973). *Teaching Science as Continuous Inquiry.* New York: McGraw-Hill.

Sadow, M. W. (1982). The use of story grammar in the designing of questions. *The Reading Teacher,* 35:5 518–522.

ADDITIONAL REFERENCES

Craik, F. I., & Watkins, M. J. (1973). The role of rehearsal in short-term memory. *Journal of Verbal Learning and Verbal Behavior, 12,* 599–607.

Gambrell, L. B., Koskinen, P. S., & Kapinus, B. (1985, December). Retelling as an instructional strategy for elementary school children. Paper presented at the National Reading Conference, San Diego, Calif.

Gambrell, L., Pfeiffer, W., & Wilson, R. (1985). The effects of retelling upon reading comprehension and recall of text information. *Journal of Educational Research,* 78, 216–220.

Ornstein, P. A., & Naus, M. J. (1978). Rehearsal processes in children's memory. In P. A. Ornstein (Ed.), *Memory development in children.* Hillsdale, N.J.: Erlbaum.

Taylor, B. M. (1982). A summarizing strategy to improve middle grade students' reading and writing skills. *The Reading Teacher, 36,* 202–205.

Comprehension Instruction with Special Groups

8

At least three groups of students need special consideration when teachers make decisions about reading comprehension instruction:

- Students who cannot comprehend from materials written at the level of their grade placement in school (remedial readers)
- Students for whom English is a second language (ESL)
- Students who are highly able

While labels do not usually serve a helpful function for students, they do help us to discuss special students who need special considerations for reading comprehension instruction. The problem with the labels is that they tend to focus our attention upon one characteristic of the student and might cause us to ignore other characteristics that might, if we attended to them, be important in our decision making regarding those students. But in order to discuss these students, we'll take the risks involved, as long as the reader remembers the limitations of labels.

REMEDIAL READERS

These students can receive a variety of labels: remedial readers, learning disabled, dyslexic, handicapped, and so on. We'll use the label *remedial readers*. They cannot profit from comprehension instruction from most of the materials that are available to the teacher at their grade placement. While adjustment of materials and instructional strategies might be made during reading instruction, these students are likely to spend much of the school day in frustrating situations. This is especially true in the upper elementary grades, when instruction in the content subjects leaves the teacher with few options. In our reading clinic we try to work with these upper elementary-age remedial reading students in content areas as much as possible because we realize that in their school placements they will need to be able to function in the content areas as comprehenders.

So there is hope, and we'll take a look at some of the options teachers can choose to help these students be successful comprehenders.

1.   Teachers might first want to spend some time on prereading activities to ensure that the students have developed the appropriate prior knowledge necessary for the content to be understood. Many students who are reading below grade level lack the necessary reading experiences to have adequate prior knowledge to benefit from instruction. While direct instruction provides some of that prior knowledge, most able readers acquire such knowledge through wide reading. Since these students do not read widely, they have the need for planned experiences to develop prior knowledge in many areas.

Prereading activities could involve the teacher's reading to the students from materials they have missed, showing film strips or motion pictures, or simply providing for a discussion before reading. For example, if a lesson were to be on the understanding of termite colonies, a film about termites might be appropriate. Or a discussion about how termites live and how they cause problems could be helpful. Most remedial readers feel very uncomfortable when reading unfamiliar content. (And not only remedial readers—all of us feel the same discomfort. Prior knowledge really helps us comprehend what is to be read. Without such knowledge, we feel frustrated. For example, have you ever tried to understand the value of the U.S. dollar and its impact upon your investments or your travel plans? You might be able to read all of the words about your investment or travel plans, but if you lack the knowledge about the value of the dollar, poor decisions could result.)

Class discussions are probably the easiest and sometimes the most efficient way for developing prior knowledge. By using the knowledge of others, the teacher can direct the discussion so that those who are less informed can get the needed information without the teacher's having to call to their attention what they do not know. Remedial readers might also be quite knowledgeable on some of the topics they are to read, and they can be leaders in these types of discussions.

2. Another prereading activity involves the anticipation of new vocabulary that might cause remedial readers considerable frustration. While many teachers introduce new words before reading, remedial readers might need some help with words that are not new to other readers. After skimming the material to be read, the teacher can identify some words that might cause remedial readers some problems. Once these words have been identified, the teacher can easily present those words in several contexts while reading the passage to facilitate comprehension. For example, if the teacher thought that the word *disaster* might be difficult for some remedial readers, it could be presented as follows:

The picnic was a <u>disaster</u>. Too many bees.
A <u>disaster</u> was about to happen. The big dog, Max, seemed very upset.
Sharon's dinner turned out to be a <u>disaster</u>. The steaks were burned.

In each of these contextual examples, the potentially difficult word could be underlined. The meaning or possible meanings could be discussed. Having experienced the word in several contexts enhances the possibility for that word becoming no problem for these readers. And, it only takes a minute to conduct such prereading vocabulary activities. (For other prereading vocabulary activities, see Chapter 6.)

3. When students have difficulty remembering their sight words, reading comprehension always suffers. Most remedial reading students have this difficulty retaining sight words. Instead of attending to the passage meaning they attend to the difficult words. We have found that introducing sight words with *signs* aids in their retention (Wilson & Hoyer, 1985). It works like this:

1. Show, for example, the word *jump*.
2. Sign the word: Place the first two fingers of your right hand on your left palm, suggesting legs. Now, make them jump.

Sign for jump
left hand: palm up
right hand: two fingers look
like jumping

3. As you sign the word, pronounce it.
4. Have the students repeat this procedure several times; i.e., while looking at the word, sign it and pronounce it. Review the sign every day for a couple of days until it becomes automatic.

Teachers have found signing to be easy to use, and it serves to motivate their students. Signs motivate for several reasons. They are codes, and children always like codes. They provide a meaningful multistimulation, i.e., visual, auditory, and motor. They provide an access to another world of communication, used mostly by deaf students but now accessed to these remedial reading students. Some

students who could barely remember any of their sight words were near perfect when using signs. Hafer (1985) found that children had better retention of sight vocabulary when taught through signing, as compared to the traditional method of tracing. Signing was readily accepted by the learning disabled students in this study and required much less instructional time than did tracing.

Teachers do not need to know any signs to use this strategy. They need only a book that illustrates signs. We recommend *The Comprehensive Signed English Dictionary* (Bornstein, Sauliner, & Hamilton, 1983). They might also want to obtain the booklet *Signing for Reading Success* (Hafer & Wilson, 1986).

Signing is another way to activate students' mental imagery. It changes the learning process, placing meaning (the sign for *jump*) ahead of pronunciation. Most signs are like the sign for *jump* in that they are iconic: They carry meaning by the way the signs are made. For example:

Sign for up
right forefinger shows up

Sign for down
right forefinger shows down

Sign for eat
mime right hand feeding
mouth

Sign for sleep
right hand rests on tilted
head

We have recently worked with teachers in two elementary schools that use signing in many areas of the curriculum. For example, in one kindergarten class, children sign as they sing the national anthem, recite the Pledge of Allegiance to the flag, and work with their numbers, colors, sizes, and shapes. The signs add a dimension of meaning otherwise not available. For example, after signing while pledging allegiance to the flag, these kindergarten children were able to discuss the meaning of each section; the signs helped them to understand the meaning of the words. In another school the special education class signed while they sang their song at the Holiday Sing. They were proud to know something the other children did not; moreover, they knew the meaning of the words in the song.

4. Another prereading strategy involves a teacher's awareness of the need for students to have purposes for their reading; this need is most acute for remedial readers. Whether set by the teacher or by the students, the purposes for the reading activity should be very clear. Purposes can be set for very short sections of the passage. Once read, these short sections can be discussed and new purposes can be established. More mature readers' purposes should be established for larger units of print, of course.

Some teachers allow good readers to establish their own purposes but take on the job themselves for remedial readers. It is understandable that some teachers do not think that remedial readers can set reasonable purposes. However, we have found that remedial readers in our clinic do very well at setting purposes. A teacher might start by giving them several purposes from which to choose. This serves as a modeling activity. The teacher can use a think-aloud strategy and say, "I wonder what this story is going to be about? The story title is *Climbing High Mountains*. I'm eager to read this story to find out where these mountains are and who climbed them." Then the teacher can give the students opportunities for choosing their own purposes, using story titles, pictures, or information from the first paragraph. In the long run, we really only read material for which we have personal purposes. Reading for the purposes set by others makes the activity seem an assignment—or a task.

5. The teacher can also attempt to adjust the difficulty of the materials to be read. In 1963 Science Research Associates developed a laboratory of reading materials that suited the interests of students but were adjusted to their reading levels. For example, the range of reading levels in the fourth grade kit was from 3 to 12. But the kit maintained a common interest for students at the fourth grade level.

This innovation suited reading instruction, and it also offered help for teachers in the content areas, since many of these passages were content based.

6. Several things can be done to help remedial readers with content materials. The teacher can read these materials into a tape recorder and have the remedial reading students use the text and the tape as a read-along activity. He or she can read the story aloud with the students or read content material to the students without their reading along. The teacher can develop study guides to help the students use the content materials efficiently.

ESL STUDENTS

As the number and diversity of ESL students increases, teachers face major problems with reading comprehension instruction. These problems include attempting to teach ESL students who have a low proficiency with English, both oral and written; students who have limited or no schooling experiences and therefore never learned to read in their own language; students without complete family units; and students who have experienced unusual suffering. These students also come from cultures that have different values and customs. Many of them are frightened and confused. Trying to learn from materials written in English often adds to their discomfort.

But all is not negative. Many of them are very bright and eager to learn. Many have strong family support systems for success in school. Almost all of them are extremely motivated to learn to communicate in English. If they are refugees, they realize that there is little likelihood that they will ever return to their homeland. They know that their chances of success in this country rest with becoming proficient in English as soon as possible.

Bilingual education has been tried with success in some areas in which there is a density of one first-language population, such as Spanish. Most teachers, however, will not have access to a bilingual program and will need to provide instruction in English with texts written in English. What is the teacher to do? Here are a few suggestions. We'll start with some suggestions for helping ESL students adjust to their new classrooms.

1. If the ESL student is severely lacking in English, try to find a student who has that first language and develop a buddy system for initial assistance. Since families often arrive in this country in groups or migrate to areas where their friends have settled, the chances of finding an ESL student with some English proficiency are good. These "buddies" can assist with orienting the new ESL students to the school. They can help them find restrooms, lunch rooms, nursing stations, telephones, and playgrounds. They can help their new friends to attach English names to these areas. They can start their new friends on some basic English, such as "no," "yes," "don't understand," and "need help." During reading instruction, they can work together until the new students gain an understanding of classroom procedures.

2. If no ESL buddy can be found, an English-speaking buddy can do many of the same things to help the ESL student in the school and in the classroom. Peers have amazing skills when asked to help one another. They tend to be patient, understanding, and nonthreatening. They can use gestures and signs to help their nonEnglish speaking friends. The English-speaking buddy can also learn some basic words from his or her new friend and aid in the translation from the first language to English. In this way, both students benefit.

3. Some schools have evaluation programs for new ESL students. They determine the English proficiency of these new students in listening, reading, writing, and speaking. This knowledge can greatly assist the teacher with initial reading instruction. Since many countries teach English as a second language, newly arrived ESL students might have some degree of English proficiency.

4. Whenever possible, a person proficient in the first language of the new student should attempt to contact the student's

home. Information about prior schooling, health needs, family intactness, siblings, etc. can be of great aid to the teacher. For example, the person might find out that the new student has better English proficiency than do the parents and that he or she serves as a translator about school matters for the parents. Such contacts also let the parents know that there is someone available with whom they can communicate in their native language.

5. When the first language is a common one like Spanish, many schools have provided instruction in that first language for the teachers, administrators, and office staff. These school personnel report the satisfaction that students and parents express when greeted in their first language. Of course, the students and parents might assume that the school personnel are fluent in their language and go into an overly rapid discussion to the frustration—and possibly also the amusement—of all involved. Teachers who can use the new ESL student's first language to some degree will find initial instruction in all areas much easier.

6. Many parents of ESL students are working hard to make a success of their opportunities in our country. They might be working two or more jobs to make ends meet. They might also be working in jobs far below their skill and education levels in their homeland. Sensitivity and awareness to these situations can be of great help. For example, asking parents to work on school volunteer projects might be unreasonable if they are working two jobs. Assuming that a new immigrant is not educated could be a mistake. We know of some college graduates from foreign countries who, initially, can find work only as domestics. While teachers cannot be responsible for these demeaning situations, they can be aware of the difficulties such situations cause the parents and be understanding of their frustrations. We know of a refugee from Cuba who had been an experienced air-traffic controller but had few English skills and, as a result, could only obtain menial labor

in this country. His frustration with his lack of English was acute; it cost him a well-paying, prestigious position. He assured us, however, that he was happy to be here, free and not bothered by an unfriendly government. He also, we are sure, wanted us to know that he had very highly refined skills. Once that was recognized, we had passed step one in terms of communication.

7. Teachers should provide home assignments that can be completed without parental help. If students arrive at the age of ten and have had no schooling, false assumptions can be made by teachers. For example, the teacher might incorrectly assume that these students know how to use pencils or scissors. Such students have had no school experience and might not understand the expectations of the school staff. They might not know what it means to meet a principal or an ESL teacher. They might have no test-taking skills, so they do not do well in testing situations.

8. Some school systems provide teachers with instructional packets to assist them in instructing ESL students. The packets provide suggestions for helping students understand schooling and the language of school. In low-impacted ESL areas such packets may not be available, but they can be obtained from almost all schools with high-impacted ESL students.

9. A welcome packet can also be prearranged by the classroom teacher or other school personnel, such as the ESL teacher. This packet might include items such as a notebook, a folder, pencil and paper, a picture dictionary, a file box, and scissors. Teachers might add things to this welcome packet as the situation demands.

10. The classroom teacher can designate an area of the classroom as an ESL lab. Special materials and activities can be placed in this area for the ESL students to use. These activities and materials can include such items as puzzles (word-pictures), handwriting activities (practicing letter

formation), audiovisual activities (audiobooks, tapes, film strips, language masters), games, magazines, library books, and workbooks.

One area of special concern is the area of testing for reading comprehension—or testing, in general. Obviously, tests normed on middle-class Americans, or on any other American group, are not valid for ESL students. Even teacher-made tests must be used cautiously in interpreting an ESL student's progress. It is in the area of testing that most ESL students might be made to look as though they were performing poorly, when in actuality they might be making satisfactory progress. Teachers should be encouraged to obtain multiple indicators of progress.

These suggestions are not meant to indicate that teachers and other school staff are insensitive to the needs of ESL students; most are sensitive. However, a teacher might make false assumptions about ESL students' situations in school because of the teacher's experiences with American students.

The task a classroom teacher faces when providing reading instruction to ESL students is a difficult one. Often there is little or no help available. We offer these suggestions possibly to ease the transition of ESL students into the American classroom, where reading comprehension instruction, which is essential to their success in our schools, is most often offered in English.

Robert Slavin, at Johns Hopkins University, and some of his associates have been looking into the effects of student team learning as an effective way to approach instruction (Slavin, 1980). While this work was conducted with mainstreamed students, it has direct implications for work with ESL students as well. Student team learning can be used in several ways. The idea is for students to work in small teams toward common objectives. All students on the team share in the learning work required and share in the evaluation of that work. Mainstreamed handicapped students seem to profit from such as instructional approach, and there seem to be no negative effects upon nonhandicapped students who work on such teams. The work reported so far has not been in the area of reading comprehension, but it seems likely that small teams could work together to develop think-links, personal outlines, and summaries as we discussed them in Chapter 6.

HIGHLY ABLE READERS

While the possibility of wasting educational opportunities for the first two groups of students is quite clear, highly able readers might also find instruction that is less than appropriate for their level of development. They might be lock-stepped into a curriculum that is boring and lacking in challenge. This normally happens when they are locked into a set of materials that does not and cannot meet their level of development. Or it can happen when a teacher is unaware of students' potential and assumes that the curriculum and materials available to regular students are also appropriate for these students.

Much has been written about instruction for the highly able readers. They are often referred to as "gifted." This section is intended to address those students who have well-developed reading comprehension abilities that are not being used in the instructional program in some classrooms. For example, a third grade student might be reading on a sixth grade level but have no instruction to challenge these advanced skills. For such a student to be paced in a program designed for students with third grade reading skills would usually be a great waste of both student and teacher time.

Usually a teacher will not have more than one or two such students in a classroom. Such students are not uncommon, however; they do not fit into the grouping patterns that teachers are accustomed to using. What is the teacher to do with them? The following suggestions are offered:

1. One consideration is pacing. Very able readers might be ready for independent work sooner than others. For example, they might be able to produce their own think-links and to develop personal outlines sooner than others. When they are ready for working independently, permit them to do so. (See Chapter 4).

2. Since these students might fit into no natural classroom

grouping, we suggest that teachers try contracting with these students. They can develop contracts about what they want to read and what they want to get from the reading with their teachers. Contracts allow for self-selection and self-pacing. While negotiated contracts need some monitoring in terms of the quality and quantity of the work accepted, most highly able readers tend to meet the terms of the contracts with responsibility and enthusiasm. Daily or weekly conferences can usually accomplish the monitoring of contracts. Contracts are best used when there is a written agreement signed by both the student and the teacher. "Signed contracts" add a sense of commitment to the task.

3. Highly able readers need group contacts with students of differing abilities, as well as individualized attention. During group instruction they can serve as role models and peer aides. For example, in the ESL section of this chapter we discussed the idea of team learning. In team learning the aspect of competition is greatly reduced and the aspect of "team spirit" can take the place of competition. Teaming helps all students to contribute to the final product, able and less able readers alike.

4. Many highly able readers can serve an important function in most classrooms: They can become tutors. Several things are known about peer tutoring. The tutor usually learns as much as or more than the student being tutored. However, being an instructor (tutor) adds demands that most students do not need to face: complete understanding of the lesson to be taught, absolute familiarity with the materials being used, and compassion for the learner being helped (Koskinen & Wilson, 1982).

5. Most highly able readers have become fine reading comprehenders on their own because they see reading as an enjoyable free-time activity. This does not mean, however, that they are not in need of direct instruction. For example, they might be able to read and understand their text but not have any idea about how to express their new knowl-

edge. They might need a lot of help with report writing, summarizing, and retelling. Just because they are highly able readers does not mean that they have the reporting strategies needed to communicate their advanced abilities. Teachers will need to help them when these strategies are needed. (See Chapter 4.)

CHAPTER SUMMARY

While most of the comprehension strategies presented in the pre-ceeding chapters are appropriate for all students, there are some special considerations for special groups. In this chapter those special considerations are suggested for (1) remedial readers, (2) students for whom English is a second language, and (3) highly able students. Teachers will find these students in their classes and will need to make adjustments for them to be comprehenders of text.

REFERENCES

Bornstein, H., Sauliner, K., & Hamilton, L. (1983), *The Comprehensive Signed English Dictionary*. Washington, DC: Gallaudet College Press.

Hafer, J. (1985). The effects of signing as a multisensory technique for teaching sight vocabulary to learning disabled hearing students. Unpublished doctoral disser-tation, University of Maryland.

Hafer, J., & Wilson, R. (1986). *Signing for Reading Success*. Washington, DC: Gallaudet College Press.

Koskinen, P. S., & Wilson, R. M. (1982). *A Guide for Student Tutors*. New York: Teachers College Press.

Slavin, R. E. (1980). Effects of student teams and peer tutoring on academic achieve-ment and time on task. *Journal of Experimental Education*, 48, 252–257.

Wilson R., & Hoyer, J. (1985). The use of signing as a reinforcement of sight vocabulary in the primary grades. *State of Maryland IRA Yearbook*, State of Maryland IRA.

Materials for Reading Comprehension

9

This chapter will discuss the materials that teachers might use for reading comprehension instruction. While materials for instruction have been mentioned in other chapters, this chapter will emphasize the following materials, with suggestions about their advantages and limitations:

1. Basal readers
2. Trade books
3. Content area textbooks
4. Reference books
5. Newspapers and magazines
6. Functional reading materials
7. Kits and special books

BASAL READERS

Basal readers are the most used materials for teaching all aspects of reading, including reading comprehension. These materials come with multiple copies of texts for students, a teacher's guide, materials for follow-up activities, and other supplementary materials, such as placement tests, skill competency tests, and checklists. Some school systems purchase the complete set of materials, while others select only certain materials from the set.

Teacher's guides usually provide suggestions for teachers in the following areas: (1) suggestions for preparing students for the reading activity, (2) suggestions for assisting students during the reading of the text, and (3) suggestions for follow-up and enrichment activities. These guides usually offer more suggestions than teachers can use, so teachers will need to select the suggestions that are most appropriate for their students.

While the students' texts are designed for various levels of readers, such as 2-1 for the first half of second grade and 2-2 for the second half of second grade, most of these texts contain materials that might be too easy or too difficult for given students at those grade placements. Of course, grade placement does not mean that students in that grade are reading on grade level. Further, there is great variability in the level of materials within any designated grade-level basal reading. For example, a text designed for readers at the first half of third grade might contain text in some of the stories that have readability at the fourth grade level and some at the second grade level (Eberwein, 1979). Basal authors elect to do this in order to present interesting text for the readers. Teachers need to be aware of these readability variations so that they can best assist their students.

Most basals look very much alike. While some stress different activities at the various levels, they all present similar activities for the students to use as they develop their reading comprehension abilities. For example, they all include activities to assist students with the development of critical reading, understanding the main idea, and noting important sequences. They might do so at different levels in the basals, but they all do so.

Publishing companies have recently published basal readers that are much better in terms of story quality. Some of the early basals contained stories that had little to hold student interest. Stories were contrived to control vocabulary and skill development, and they resulted in stilted, unnatural-sounding language. They lost student interest, and without student interest, reading comprehension is almost impossible to teach. Many students became bored and were unable to comprehend these materials, so most publishers have upgraded the quality of the literature they use in their basals.

Basal follow-up materials have received considerable criticism. They often involve the use of workbooks or dittos. At times they are very contrived, having little or nothing to do with the text that has just been read. Since the costs of these follow-up materials can be considerable, school systems should examine them carefully before investing in them. If they have been purchased, teachers should be permitted to use them selectively. That is, they should not be expected to use them just because they are available. They should use them when the material fits their instructional objectives. Otherwise, teachers should consider using some of the other materials being presented in the remainder of this chapter.

Some school systems require teachers to follow the basal teacher's guide closely. This requirement is made for at least two reasons. First, school systems that have high student mobility—that is, students move from one school to another within the system—want to have program continuity for the mobile students. The other obvious reason is that a school system might have a large group of inexperienced teachers who need a stable program. It seems to us, however, that teachers should not be required to teach reading from materials with which they are uncomfortable or have basic problems concerning the approaches or strategies being suggested. It seems likely that teachers will do the best job with comprehension instruction when they are using materials with which they are comfortable and with which they can best use their teaching skills.

When teachers are the final decision makers, decisions involving teaching comprehension strategies or decisions about how to use basal readers to facilitate comprehension should usually result in the desired instructional environment. In the remainder of this chapter, we suggest some other decisions that teachers need to make about materials for the best possible reading comprehension instruction.

TRADE BOOKS

Trade books are books available to the public, as compared to basal readers and content area textbooks. Some trade books are literature books for children; others are books on special topics. They involve students in whole book reading. They can be found in media centers, in public libraries, and in bookstores. It is hoped that they can also be found in every elementary classroom. Teachers can use trade books to supplement their students' reading activities. For example, if the students have just completed a reading activity involving space exploration and are very excited about the topic, the teacher might help them select trade books on space exploration for their free-time reading. Some teachers set aside specific times during the week for recreational reading of trade books. This use of time during school serves several purposes: It helps students to learn that reading is viewed as an important and enjoyable activity, provides practice with silent reading, and helps to develop reading as a free-time habit. We have all known students who have learned to read but do not choose to read as a free-time activity. By providing school time for recreational reading, teachers provide such students with the opportunity to experience the enjoyment of reading. When all school reading time is used for completing assignments, some students may view reading as a chore; therefore, they will not choose to read for enjoyment. Most teachers also read during these free times, helping to set a model for the students: They see that their teacher is a reader. The teacher can also use the time to read some of the books the students are reading.

Some teachers have each student keep a trade book in his or her desk. The students are instructed that they can read their books whenever they are finished with their required activities. Many students waste time in school when they finish an activity and are waiting for teacher directions. By getting into the habit of reading from their trade book during these times, students can realize the same benefits mentioned above when teachers provide specified reading time during school.

At times teachers will want to know what their students are learning from their free-time reading. Traditionally, teachers have used book reports to get this information. At times, book reports can turn free-time reading into an unpleasant activity. Teachers should be aware of the negative possibilities that can result from book-report writing. They might want to consider one of the following alternatives:

1. Have a brief conference with the students to discuss what they have been reading.
2. Have students draw pictures of the event they thought most interesting.
3. Have students orally share interesting events from their reading.
4. Have students complete an advertisement for the book they have completed. These can be written on a $3'' \times 5''$ index card and stored in a file box for other students to read, thus creating interest in reading the book or story.
5. Have students make think-links or personal outlines about characters or events that were interesting to them. (See Chapter 4.)

While we believe that students should learn to write good reports, we offer these suggestions as alternatives to report writing to add variety to activities involved with recreational reading. Of course, most of the time, recreational reading should be done with no type of reporting required; that is the way we all enjoy reading for recreation.

CONTENT AREA TEXTBOOKS

Reading to get information from content area textbooks can be quite a different activity from reading to get information from basal readers or trade books. Teachers will therefore need to plan specific instruction when introducing students to content area reading.

Content area textbooks have two characteristics that might cause problems for many students. First, they are usually written by authors who are not very concerned about the readability level of the text. In order for them to present the content that is needed, they often raise the readability level of the text. So a fourth grade social studies text might well have sections that are written two or three grade levels above the fourth grade level. Second, there is a real possibility that a lot of new concepts will occur in various sections of the text. This is called concept density. The concept density of a science book written for fifth graders might be very great when the author is introducing, for example, a section on the types of clouds one can observe. Similarly, even proficient adult readers have a problem with concept density when reading legal documents: Their problem is not with the word difficulty, but with the concepts those words carry; when there are too many concepts in a paragraph, the reader becomes confused. So it is with elementary students when they start reading in an area about whose concepts they have little or no prior knowledge.

Another concern about content area textbook reading is the retention of what is read. If students are reading stories in their basal readers or their trade books, there might not be much concern about whether the information read is remembered over time. In content reading, however, there is usually some expectation that some of that information will be retained in memory. Story reading (narrative) and content reading (expository) vary in their importance for being remembered.

What are teachers to do?

1. They can prepare students for new concepts by introducing these concepts through pictures, examples, and student discussion. When these new concepts are met in text, they will not be so new.
2. They can be aware of readability difficulties and help students by introducing new words before the reading of the text. New words then do not become such a threat to the readers. When new words are a threat, the students tend to concentrate upon the words and not the information to be understood; without that threat, they can concentrate on comprehension of the passage.
3. They can help students to understand what authors have included to aid them with their reading. They can help them to use the illustrations, pictures, underlining, highlightings, and captions to be better able to read the texts. Authors include these text features to facilitate comprehension.
4. They can help students read content area texts by developing study guides (Herber, 1978; Graham & Robinson,

1984). Study guides let students know what to look for in their reading of content texts. What questions need to be answered? Where might those answers be found? What do the authors provide by way of captions and illustrations? Study guides can help all students make the best use of text.

5. They can instruct students to use efficient study techniques. There are several such techniques available for use; the most common one is SQ3R (S = survey, Q = question, R = read, R = recite, R = review [Robinson, 1961]). Most elementary school students do not receive such instruction, so they develop their own study systems or they study without any system at all. Self-developed systems are often not very effective; yet students tend to stick with them whether or not they are effective.

Helping students to understand content area textbooks and helping them to learn from them must be a priority for elementary school teachers. Without help, students are often not able to use these texts effectively. Waiting until students develop their own strategies for study from content books makes learning other effective strategies more difficult. We have learned that it is better to teach effective systems early, as soon as students are expected to study independently.

REFERENCE BOOKS

As needs emerge for the use of additional information, students will be referring to reference materials that can be found in and out of the classroom. Most reference materials will be found in media centers in the schools and in libraries outside the schools. These reference materials include encyclopedias, technical journals, atlases, and other such sources of information. Some students cannot use these materials effectively without instruction.

Teachers can ask media specialists to help with the introduction of the various reference materials available in the school. These introductions can be supplemented by in-class suggestions for the use of reference materials. We have found that often even college students are unskilled in the use of such materials. Asking students to use reference materials without specific instruction requires them to develop their own strategies, just as they might have to do with content area textbooks. Because of their lack of experience in the use of reference materials, many students develop an avoidance response; that is, they try to get information from other sources because the task of using these strange materials appears to be too difficult. A carefully planned and systematic introduction can save many hours of frustration and save many poorly prepared reports.

NEWSPAPERS AND MAGAZINES

The use of newspapers and magazines for reading comprehension instruction is often overlooked, but the potential for highly motivating instructional material is lost when they are ignored.

Newspapers provide students with up-to-date information, and they are expendable. That is, newspaper articles can be circled, marked, cut up, and pasted; if they are destroyed, it does not matter: They can easily be replaced; there will be a new one tomorrow. The American Newspaper Publishers Association (ANPA) works with newspapers to produce materials for classroom use. These materials appear in the form of workbooks, study guides, and study cards. Many of them are highly creative and are very motivating to students. ANPA also provides a periodic review of materials prepared by the various newspapers for use in the classroom (*Newspapers in Education*, 1982). The name of the ANPA newspaper program is Newspapers in Education. The Newspapers in Education program is an interesting one. Newspaper publishers are naturally concerned about having a newspaper readership population. If they do not have such a population, newspaper circulation suffers, and then many newspapers cannot survive. As a result, they invest large amounts of money to promote newspaper reading in schools. The teacher should contact his or her local newspaper to determine whether it has a Newspapers in Education program. A booklet has been prepared by ANPA to assist teachers with this instruction (Wilson & Barnes, 1979). Teachers can use newspapers as a medium for teaching some of the following comprehension skills:

1. Main idea by matching headings, which have been separated from the article, with the article and by matching photograph captions with the photographs
2. Sorting fact from opinion by contrasting the number of facts and opinions on the front page with the number on the editorial page
3. Interpreting persuasive language used in advertisements
4. Noting figurative language used in headlines on the sports pages
5. Understanding the sequence of events by following activities like a space flight or a SuperBowl game over a period of time or by putting together comic strips that have been cut into individual frames.

Instruction in these newspaper activities might first involve class-directed instruction, during which all students would complete the activities under teacher direction. Students quickly learn to work on these newspaper activities alone or in small groups, and they seem to enjoy doing so. We think they enjoy it for at least three reasons:

1. They are working with materials they see adults reading.
2. The material is current and up to date.
3. They can mark on it, cut it, and paste it. Something they cannot do in most other materials in school.

Magazines provide another source of reading comprehension materials. Like newspapers, they contain current information that might well be related to students' prior knowledge—a real asset for reading comprehension instruction. Teachers can use them for teaching many of the same skills that they can use with newspapers.

Magazines are more expensive than newspapers, but they can be obtained without cost. Most parents subscribe to one or more magazines. When they have read the magazines, they usually throw them away. A note home to ask for unused magazines can provide teachers with a rich source of reading comprehension materials. We assume, of course, that teachers will screen such magazines to exclude those with unsuitable materials for in-school instruction. In our reading clinic we use magazines like *Sports Illustrated*, *Life*, and *Chesapeake Bay Magazine*. Various faculty simply save them and bring them to the clinic instead of throwing them away. Any school could do the same thing.

FUNCTIONAL READING MATERIALS

Newspapers and magazines provide students with obvious reading materials from the real world, but teachers need to be aware of the many other sources of functional reading materials. Cereal boxes, medicine labels, local maps, bulk-mail advertisements and recipes are but a few that are readily available for in-school instruction. Not only are these materials readily available to most students, reading them might also keep students from making serious mistakes in their daily lives. For example, take a look at the label on an aspirin bottle; what should students know about the use and misuse of this medicine? Look at the promotional features of some of your own bulk mail; how could future adults make unwise decisions in responding to such promotional efforts? Is the local map detailed enough to help students find a new location for a hardware store? If it is not, where can they find better information: the yellow pages? Should they ask someone or check another source?

There is no reason for teachers to assume that their students can comprehend functional materials in the real world. Direct instruction is needed, and it cannot wait until students are out in the real world. It must start in the elementary school.

We have developed a kit of materials that can be used by teachers of all elementary grades to provide real-life reading comprehension materials for elementary instruction (Wilson & Wilson, 1980). It has activities for grades 1 through 6 in ditto format. Teachers will surely see the potential of functional reading materials after using this kit.

Teachers can, of course, use the functional reading materials available to them in their own communities. For example, menus from local restaurants, TV listings, school information, and class schedules are readily available. Information about health care needs, the best food prices, recreational facilities, and emergency room phone numbers are just a few of the materials that teachers can easily find. We suggest that the teacher look around his or her local community to determine what students might need for local functional reading. At a broader level, there are functional reading activity needs beyond the local community level, for example, statewide maps, the menus of unfamiliar restaurants, labels for prescription medicines, and national advertisements, to mention a few. Some teachers collect such materials on their vacations and save them for functional reading activities. For example, did you ever notice those interesting paper placemats in inexpensive restaurants or those travel folders in hotel and motel lobbies?

KITS AND SPECIAL BOOKS

There are other materials available to teachers for reading comprehension instruction. These include, but are not limited to, kits and special books. Science Research Associates first introduced multilevel kits for instruction in the late 1960s. Since then, many publishers have developed kits to aid teachers. To mention a few: (1) *National Football League Kit*, by Bowmar/Noble, (2) *Guinness Book of World Records Kit*, by Singer, and (3) *The Literature Sampler*, by Learning Materials. Don't they sound like a lot of fun? There are a lot of them out there; keep your eyes peeled for them. Such kits usually provide teachers with high-interest materials for reading comprehension activities.

These kits are usually used as a supplement to direct teacher instruction. They can be used by students as independent activities, since they require little teacher direction. The high interest level of many of these kits helps to hold student attention.

The teacher will need to examine the nature of the comprehension activities to determine whether they are suitable for the students' skill level. Teachers will find many of these kits contain large amounts of literal comprehension activities. Teacher might direct their students to select alternate activities instead of those presented in the kit materials. Some of the comprehension strategies discussed in Chapters 3 and 4 of this book could be used. For example, instead of answering the literal questions included with the materials, the teacher might have students make personal outlines on points of interest. Or the teacher might have students make think-links about their favorite characters. Students can also use the activities suggested under the section on trade books in this chapter. Students seem to enjoy working with these materials when there is some variety in the after-reading activities.

Some publishers provide teachers with special books designed to aid the reading comprehension process. To name a few: (1) *The Monster Book*, by Bowmar/Noble, (2) *Getting the Main Idea*, by Barnell Loft, and (3) *Troll I Can Read Series*, by Troll Associates. These books might be directed toward certain comprehension subskills, such as locating information or reading for the main idea. Teachers must determine what skill practice their students need and select the books appropriate for that practice. Of course, since these books are used mostly for independent student use, teachers need to be sure that their students have the skills required for using these books in practice activities.

Some special books are developed to provide students with interesting reading materials and various levels of difficulty. These books have the same features as the kits we just discussed. Teachers might want to consider using the suggestions we made in that section to add variety to the practice activities.

CHAPTER SUMMARY

In this chapter we have discussed some of the materials most often found in the classroom or the media center that can be used for reading comprehension activities. Since new materials are being developed on a regular basis, teachers will want to be on the lookout for the best materials that are available. The care in the development of these materials varies greatly. The teacher needs to examine each material to determine whether it is appropriate for the students and the curriculum. There are many comprehension instructional materials that are not commercially developed for instruction, but have great appeal to students and considerable educational value.

REFERENCES

Eberwein, L. D. (1979). The variability of basal reader textbooks and how much teachers know about it. *Reading World*, *18:3*, 259–272.

Graham, K., & Robinson. H. A. (1984). *Study Skills Hand Book*. Newark, Del.: International Reading Association, Ch. 2.

Herber, H. (1978). *Teaching Reading in Content Areas*. Englewood- Cliffs, N.J.: Prentice Hall, Ch. 4.

NIE (1982). *Bibliography: Newspapers in Education Publications*. Reston, Va.: American Newspaper Publishers Association.

Robinson, F. (1961). *Effective Study*. New York: Harper & Row.

Wilson, R., & Barnes, M. (1979). *Using Newspapers to Teach Reading Skills*. Reston, Va., American Newspaper Publishers Association.

Wilson, R., & Wilson, M. (1980). *Real-Life Reading*, Minneapolis, Minn.: Judy/Instructor.

Motivation: A Central Component of Reading Comprehension

10

It is generally acknowledged that motivation is a central component of the reading comprehension process (Mathewson, 1976). If students are motivated, they will *want* to pick up materials to read. Encouraging students to *choose* reading as an activity should be a primary goal of reading instruction. According to Morrow (1985), the best measure of success for a reading instructional program is the enthusiasm and frequency with which students voluntarily choose to read.

Reading with strong comprehension is perhaps best exemplified when a person is engaged in reading something that has captured their interest. Given that motivation is a powerful variable in the reading comprehension process, it is crucial that adequate time and attention be devoted to activities that are designed to motivate students to read.

There is converging evidence that students actually spend very little time reading during teacher-directed reading instruction (Gambrell, 1986a) and during the typical classroom day (Dishaw, 1977). Typically, students in first to third grades spend only two to five minutes during the teacher-directed portion of the reading lesson engaging in silent reading (Gambrell, 1986a). Across the school day, evidence shows that primary grade students engage in silent reading for only seven or eight minutes per day, and by the middle grades students spend an average of only fifteen minutes of the school day engaged in silent reading (Dishaw, 1977).

Time spent on silent reading in school is positively associated with year-to-year gains in reading achievement (Allington, 1984). There is also evidence that the amount of time students devote to reading outside school is positively related to gains in reading achievement (Fielding, Wilson, & Anderson, in press). There is no doubt that students of every age ought to be doing more extended silent reading (Anderson, Hiebert, Scott, & Wilkinson, 1985). Clearly, the reading instruction program should include attention to motivational activities that will encourage recreational reading both during and outside school.

TEACHER DECISION MAKING
AND MOTIVATION

If students are exposed to a classroom environment that associates reading with pleasure and enjoyment, it is likely that they will be motivated to engage in voluntary reading. There are many decisions concerning the instructional reading program that have an impact upon the motivational climate of the classroom. Some questions that should be considered include the following:

1. Are students exposed to literature on a daily basis?
2. Are teacher read-aloud sessions an integral part of the reading program?
3. Does the reading program include a recreational reading component?
4. Do you, the teacher, provide a model for sustained silent reading experiences?
5. Are students provided with opportunities to share books they have read with peers?

TEACHER READ-ALOUD
SESSIONS

According to Chomsky (1972) and Durkin (1966), the single most important activity for building the knowledge required for success in reading is *reading aloud to students.* Reading aloud to students is perhaps the most effective strategy that teachers can use for promoting voluntary reading. There is ample evidence that when teachers read to students, the students are motivated to do voluntary reading (Morrow, 1982; Morrow & Weinstein, 1986). Teachers frequently comment that when they read a book aloud to the class, several students will go to the library to check out the same book. Something special happens when a teacher "blesses" a book by reading it aloud.

Teachers can promote wide reading by sharing books with students during teacher read-aloud sessions. It is important that we remember that reading aloud is an important way of motivating students of *all* ages. While we believe that it is important for the teacher to read aloud to students every day, it is also important that variety be reflected in the teacher read-aloud sessions. Here are some suggestions for implementing an effective teacher read-aloud program designed to motivate students to engage in volunteer reading.

1. Frequently choose books, stories or articles that can be completed in a fifteen- or twenty-minute period. This is especially important in the middle and upper elementary grades where the type of material most often selected for reading aloud is a book that consists of a number of chapters and must be read over a period of weeks. It is important to model for students that there are many good books and stories that can be enjoyed and finished in a brief period. Some excellent selections that take only one session to complete can be found in folktales and picture books, such as *One Fine Day* and *The Duchess Bakes a Cake.* For older elementary students, teachers can choose from collections of short stories, sophisticated folktales, and magazine articles of an informational nature that would be appropriate for reading aloud.

2. Periodically choose a chapter book that requires several days or so to complete. Chapter books are divided into brief chapters, or they can be divided into sections to be read over an extended period of time. One note of caution: Students frequently lose interest in an excellent book if the reading is spread out over too long a period of time. One possible solution to this problem would be to have two teacher read-aloud sessions per day so that the book can be completed in a reasonable length of time. It is important, however, to model during teacher read-aloud sessions that some of the best books require a commitment over a period of time and that sometimes we *want* to choose a book we can enjoy reading over a long period.

3. Read a potpourri of books. One day a week should be set aside for sharing a variety of books with the class during the teacher read-aloud time. Instead of reading one book or a chapter from a book, collect a range of books to share: a few very easy books, perhaps a wordless picture book, a few books of medium difficulty, and perhaps a challenging book or two. There should also be a range in types of books selected; fiction, informational, folktales, and poetry are a few examples. Tell the students that you are going to share "just a bit" of some special books with them. Then proceed to read aloud the title and some selected portion or just the opening paragraph of the book. Try to end on a high point and tell the students that if they would like to know the rest of the story, they can find the book on the library table. In a fifteen- or twenty-minute period seven or eight books can be shared with students in this manner. At the conclusion all the books can be placed on the library table.

4. Remember to include expository and informational materials that are of high interest in teacher read-aloud sessions. Most students choose narrative fiction for pleasure reading; interestingly, recent research indicates that teachers overwhelmingly choose fiction when reading aloud to students (Gambrell, 1986b). One way to encourage an interest in nonfiction materials is to share them during read-aloud time. There are many good sources of this type of material, such as articles in students' magazines, informational books, biographies, and autobiographies.

RECREATIONAL READING

The goal of any recreational reading program is to produce students who choose to read because they want to read. Developing and instilling in young students a love of reading is too important to be left to chance. A well-planned recreational reading program is an important component of any reading curriculum. In this section three ways in which teachers can provide recreational reading opportunities for students will be presented: (1) read-and-think corner, (2) sustained silent reading, and (3) free reading as a follow-up activity to teacher-directed reading instruction.

Read-and-Think Corner

A read-and-think corner in the classroom can provide a place for students to "get away from it all" with a good book. A read-and-think corner can be set up in any nook or cranny in the classroom. Make it pleasant and comfortable: Find an old easy chair or a rocking chair and a small rug to use. There should be lots of reading material, a timer of some kind, and possibly a curtain or bookcase to provide privacy.

You may want to give the students in your classroom the opportunity to go to the read-and-think corner at any time they choose. All students have times when they become bored or frustrated in the classroom. Instead of distracting or disrupting the group or simply daydreaming, students might choose the option of going to the read-and-think corner to spend some time with a good book. If a student has a disagreement with a classmate, encourage the student to spend some time with a good book as a good way to "cool off." The read-and-think corner can provide students with a positive way of removing themselves from unpleasant classroom situations whenever there is a need.

In the beginning it might be advantageous to establish a time limit of possibly five or ten minutes, depending on the age of the students. A sand timer is quiet and easy for younger students to use. Older students may use a clock and a sign-in sheet on which they write the time they arrived and the time they left, along with a note about what they read.

In the busy world of the classroom the read-and-think corner provides an opportunity for a student to be alone with a favorite book. It has been our experience that students quickly learn to value their read-and-think corner and are not inclined to abuse it through excessive use.

Sustained Silent Reading

Sustained silent reading (SSR) is a practice that involves setting aside a specific amount of time each day for independent silent read-

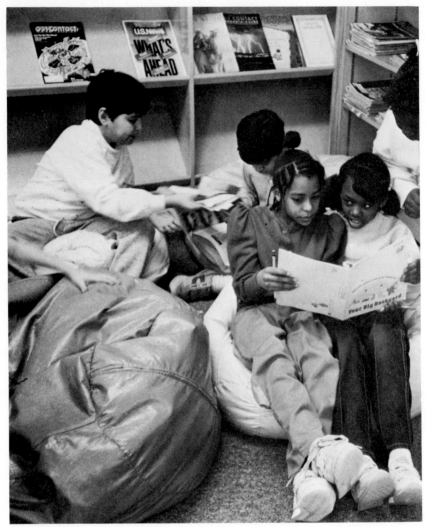

Dr. David Williams

ing. Students read whatever they choose, and so does the teacher. SSR focuses on the reading strengths and interests of students because it lets them read to satisfy themselves. Following SSR there are no activities to check to see who read what or questions to assess how well the reader has comprehended. During SSR, reading is done for self-satisfaction. The purpose is to give students time to read during the school day; the expected outcome is that students will develop the habit of choosing reading as a free-time activity.

There are three important objectives for an SSR program. The first is to provide students with time to engage in silent reading. The second is to provide students with models of sustained silent reading. The third objective is to increase students' abilities to sustain silent reading for longer periods of time.

Commonsense notions about the reading process tell us that independent reading skills are enhanced through daily practice in silent reading and that independent reading should be the primary focus of all reading programs. Observational research to date suggests that most students receive very little opportunity to engage in SSR during the school day (Dishaw, 1977; Gambrell, 1986a). SSR can be the component of the reading program that gives students the opportunity to practice their reading skills during a pleasurable, independent reading experience.

In order to implement a successful SSR program, an adequate quantity and wide range of reading materials must be available to students. Research suggests that students in classrooms with collections of books and library corners have more positive attitudes toward reading and make greater gains in reading comprehension than do students in classrooms where books are not readily available (Morrow & Weinstein, 1986). Research also suggests that the frequency with which students engage in voluntary reading both in and out of school depends upon the priority that the classroom teacher gives to independent reading (Fielding, Wilson, & Anderson, 1986).

SSR cannot work without a lot of books and other reading materials of all shapes, sizes, and levels of difficulty. Huck (1976) has suggested that six to eight books per student should be available for a classroom library. In addition to trade books and content books, make use of newspapers, magazines, comic books, student-produced books, discarded basals, and the many free and inexpensive reading materials that are readily available. One way to build a classroom library is to send a note home to parents explaining SSR and requesting donations of books and magazines (especially children's magazines). Teachers report that classroom libraries are greatly improved by these donations. One student's castaway is another student's reading treasure!

Additional reading materials can be created by cutting apart old basal readers and content books to make individual stories. With a little imagination and creativity a classroom teacher can create an extensive classroom library with a marvelous range of high-interest reading materials for SSR.

Implementing SSR. SSR is a total-class activity. Everyone reads silently during the time allotted to SSR, even the teacher. Students choose the material they want to read from the room library or the school library, or they read something they have brought from home. Students need to have their reading materials identified *before* the SSR period begins each day. If they do not, much of the time set aside for reading during SSR will be spent shuffling through materials to find something to read. This problem can be virtually eliminated by establishing a short period earlier in the day for selecting materials for SSR. When students first arrive in the morning or right before lunch, set aside five or ten minutes for this important activity.

Another area of importance in establishing a successful SSR program is helping students learn to select materials that they *can* read. The most important step here is to be certain that a wide range of books is available: lots of picture books, easy-to-read books, and magazines.

For SSR to be most effective, a daily dose of the activity is recommended. Choose a time of day that will be relatively quiet. The length of the SSR period is also important. Botel (1977) recommends that teachers begin with short periods of time and gradually extend the length of the SSR period. He suggests starting with three to five minutes at the kindergarten/primary levels. Middle elementary grades might start with ten- to fifteen-minute periods. As students become comfortable with SSR, the length of the period can be extended.

Some tips to assure success with SSR. It is very important that the teacher read during SSR. The teacher provides an important model during the activity. When the teacher does not participate, the program does not work well. For example, if you feel the need to correct papers and decide not to read, some students may feel that they have the same right to work at another activity. Set a good example. Show that you value reading by always reading during SSR.

Some students will exhibit inappropriate behavior during SSR.

Some students will test the system: They may engage in talking or doing assignments. Try to ignore their divergent behavior. After the SSR period, emphasize the rule that everyone must read during SSR. You may even want to stop the activity and stress the idea that SSR is a privilege. Let the students decide whether they can continue. Usually students are eager to have SSR and will exert peer pressure to quell inappropriate behavior during SSR.

Some students will want to share with you or with classmates what they have read during SSR. Let them. Encourage book sharing. The point is, however, sharing is not required. You will certainly want to show interest in what students have read if they come to you with enthusiasm. You might even establish some sharing time during the day for those students who want to share their excitement about a book with you or with others.

Learning to read is probably most effectively accomplished when a student is hooked on a good book. Few would argue the point that students learn to read by reading. SSR is intended to provide the reader with opportunities to become a better reader by reading and seeing others read. SSR is a simple yet effective technique for encouraging independent silent reading.

Free Reading as a Follow-Up to Teacher-Directed Reading

During the time typically allotted to reading instruction students spent approximately 70 percent of that time on independent seatwork and only 30 percent of the time in teacher-directed reading instruction (Fisher, Berliner, Filby, et al., 1978). Given the significant amount of time that students spend involved in independent seatwork during instructional reading time, it is crucial that the activities that are used during this time promote reading. The most frequently assigned task during independent seatwork time is completion of workbook pages or skill sheets. Analyses of workbook activities indicate that students are rarely provided opportunities to engage in extended reading and that only a perfunctory level of reading is required to complete the typical workbook activity. In fact, many workbook activities drill students on skills that have little value in learning to read. Recent research indicates that the amount of time devoted to worksheets is unrelated to year-to-year gains in reading achievement (Fisher, Berliner, Filby, et al., 1978). Certainly there are many well-conceived workbook activities and skill sheets that provide practice in important aspects of reading. However, the fact that so much of the reading instructional time is devoted to independent seatwork suggests that we should optimize this time to provide students with opportunities to engage in voluntary reading activities.

The following list details voluntary reading activities that can be incorporated into the independent seatwork time:

1. Allow students to read a book (or newspaper, magazine, etc.) as part of the independent seatwork time. If you designate part of the seatwork period as time for voluntary reading, this will clearly indicate that voluntary reading is valued.

2. Following teacher-directed reading instruction of a story, encourage students to read related books. Have the school librarian assist you in finding books that are related to the materials used for teacher-directed reading instruction. Encourage students to read these materials during independent seatwork time. For example, if the basal story is about an American hero, students could be encouraged to read other stories about the hero or stories about other famous American heroes or heroines during the seatwork period. Displaying these books on a small table would encourage students to choose voluntary reading as a follow-up activity. A valuable related activity would be to have the students in the reading group go to the library to select books related to the instructional story, and display them on the library table. For example, if the instructional story was based upon a fable, the students in the group could go to the library to find a collection of fables to display on the library table. Students could be encouraged to choose to read another fable as seatwork and a few minutes of the next teacher-directed reading lesson could be devoted to sharing the fables read during the seatwork time.

3. Provide writing activities for seatwork that are related to

the stories and materials that are being used for teacher-directed reading instruction. Here are some examples of activities that are related to the instructional material and require rereading, which provides practice and promotes fluent reading, written expression, and higher-level thinking and composing skills:

- Have students use their basal story or group language experience story to write questions to ask each other or, even better, to ask you. Students enjoy "testing" the teacher. When students must compose questions, they must reread the material and identify important concepts. Be sure that you ask the students for questions about *important* parts of the story so that they focus on important ideas rather than on insignificant details.
- Students can draw a picture of their favorite character in the story and write a paragraph to describe that character.
- Students can write a paragraph describing the most exciting (saddest, happiest, strangest, etc.) event in the story.
- Students can write True–False statements about the story.
- When the first half of a story has been read, the students can write an ending for the story.

With all seatwork activities of this nature that are related to the instructional material it is important to have students share their work with the group.

STUDENT BOOK SHARING

Students are frequently motivated to read a certain book when they notice that a classmate is excited about it. Book-sharing projects and activities provide students with information about many books they might find appealing. Providing students with choices concerning how they share the books they have read can make the difference between the old "book report" routine and book sharing that is fun and exciting.

Name _____				
CATEGORY	DATE	BOOK TITLE	DATE	BOOK TITLE
Fantasy	5/15	*Charlotte's Web*	6/15	*Stuart Little*
History				
Historical Fiction	5/21	*The Matchlock Gun*		
Science				
Science Fiction				
Biographies				
Poetry	6/11	*Hailstones and Halibut Bones*		

A Category Chart

Not every student can write a report to communicate how he or she felt about a book. Why not let students choose the way they want to share their books? They might make a comic strip about the book, write a newspaper article about an exciting incident, or come to class dressed as a favorite character and answer questions from the class.

To provide students with choices about what they read you might set up a category system to illustrate all the possibilities and to encourage reading in different areas.

Students can add their own categories as they read in areas of special interest, such as animal stories or witch stories. By simply filling in the date the book is completed and the title, the students provide the teacher with valuable information about their reading habits. If the teacher notices, for example, that the class reads very little historical fiction, that might be a cue to introduce some historical

name _____

Read Around the Literature Wheel

Color in a circle when you finish reading a book.

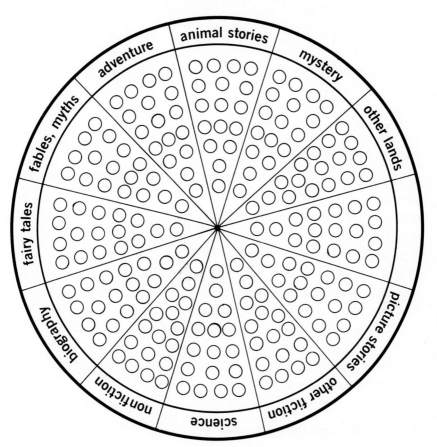

How balanced is your wheel?

fiction during a teacher read-aloud session to encourage reading in that area.

Students can also choose how they want to share their books. They often think of original and creative ways to share their reading. Providing a list of alternatives for book sharing allows students to choose an activity that appeals to them and that they can do successfully. In the following section suggestions are given for student book-sharing projects in four areas:

1. Art
2. Group interests
3. Conferences
4. Special projects

Sharing Through Art

The classroom can become an art gallery as students share books by making art projects that depict their stories. Here are several art projects from which students could choose:

1. Make puppets to dramatize your story.
2. Design and make a poster to advertise your book.
3. Construct a miniature stage setting for your story.
4. Draw a portrait of your favorite character.
5. Make a wall mural showing all the major characters in your book.
6. Make a mobile using pictures that show exciting events in your book.

Sharing Through Group Interests

When several students have read the same books, there are many ways they can share their interests. They might choose to share their books through activities like the following:

1. Divide into groups according to book sections or chapters to write a script for a play.

2. Develop a "Book Quiz." Each student prepares a written quiz of five or ten questions and puts the answers on the back of the sheet. Students can swap quiz sheets with each other and answer the questions.
3. When several students have read informational books, they can get together to demonstrate and share information related to their books. For example, groups of students could get together to demonstrate science experiments, to share rock collections or insect collections.
4. When several students have read books from a common category, they can get together to discuss literary qualities. For example, when several students have read mystery stories, they can get together to decide which one has, for example, the eeriest plot or the most mysterious character.

Sharing Through Conferences

Book conferences provide another alternative for sharing books. This can be done in a one-to-one relationship: teacher and student, or two students. Here are some suggestions for topics that can become the focus of a book conference:

1. Compare the setting of your book with your own environment.
2. Think of a different ending for your story.
3. Tell about the part of your book that was the most exciting, the funniest, the saddest, or the most interesting.
4. Describe what you would tell your friend if you wanted your friend to read this book.
5. Compare and contrast this book with one you have previously read.
6. Explain the illustrations, maps, or sketches in your book.

Sharing Through Special Projects

A way to bring special excitement to book sharing is to have the class engage in a special project such as a book fair, a costume party, or a class newspaper. All of these projects provide avenues for book sharing. Here are a few examples of book-sharing alternatives that could be developed from a class newspaper project:

1. Write a book review for the newspaper based on the book you have just read. Tell what your book is about and why others should or should not read it.
2. Draw a series of pictures for the comic strip section of the paper showing the main events of your book.
3. Write an article about the most exciting incident in your book. Make a headline and draw a picture to accompany your article.
4. Design a book jacket for your book and include it in an advertisement to entice others to read your book.
5. Pretend you are the author. Write an article telling other people why they should read your book.

CHAPTER SUMMARY

This chapter has focused upon motivational strategies and techniques for encouraging students to choose reading as an activity of personal choice. The teacher plays a critical role in motivating students to read. Three areas in which teachers play an important role were identified: teacher read-aloud sessions, providing opportunities for student book sharing, and providing opportunities for recreational reading. One of the keys to motivating students to read is a teacher who values reading and is enthusiastic about sharing a love of reading with the students. If a teacher associates reading with enjoyment, pleasure and learning, students are likely to become voluntary lifelong readers.

REFERENCES

Allington, R. (1984). Content coverage and contextual reading in reading groups. *Journal of Reading Behavior, 16*, 85–96.

Anderson, R. C., Hiebert, E. H., Scott, J. A., & Wilkinson, I.A.G. (1985). *Becoming a Nation of Readers: The Report of the Commission on Reading.* Washington, D.C.: The National Institute of Education.

Botel, M. (1977). *A Comprehensive Reading Communication Arts Plan*. Harrisburg, Pa.: Pennsylvania Department of Education.

Chomsky, C. (1972). Stages in language development and reading. *Harvard Educational Review, 42*, 1–33.

Dishaw, M. (1977). Descriptions of allocated time to content areas for the A-B period (Beginning Teacher Evaluation Study Tech. Note IV–11a). San Francisco, Calif.: Far West Regional Laboratory for Educational Research and Development.

Durkin, D. (1966). *Children Who Read Early: Two Longitudinal Studies*. New York: Teachers College Press.

Fielding, L. G., Wilson, P. T., & Anderson, R. C. (1986). A new focus on free reading: The role of trade books in reading instruction. In T. E. Raphael & R. Reynolds (Eds.) *Contexts of literacy*. New York: Longman.

Fisher, C. W., Berlinger, D., Filby, N., Marliave, R., Cohen, L., Dishaw, M., & Moore, J. (1978). Teaching and learning in elementary schools: A summary of the beginning teacher evaluation study. San Francisco, Calif.: Far West Regional Laboratory for Educational Research and Development.

Gambrell, L. B. (1986a). Reading in the primary grades: How often, how long? In M. R. Sampson (Ed.) *The Pursuit of Literacy*. Dubuque, Iowa: Kendall/Hunt.

Gambrell, L. B. (1986b, April). Reading aloud to children: Teacher's choices. Paper presented at the meeting of the International Reading Association, Philadelphia.

Huck, S. (1976). *Children's Literature in the Elementary School*. New York: Holt, Rinehart & Winston.

Mathewson, G. (1976). The function of attitudes in the reading process. In H. Singer & R. Ruddell (Eds.) *Theoretical models and processes of reading*. Newark, Del.: International Reading Association.

Morrow, L. M. (1982). Relationships between literature programs, library corner designs and children's use of literature. *Journal of Educational Research. 76*, 221–230.

Morrow, L. M. (1985). *Promoting voluntary reading in school and home*. Bloomington, Ind.: Phi Delta Kappa Educational Foundation.

Morrow, L. M., & Weinstein, C. S. (1986). Encouraging voluntary reading: The impact of a literature program on children's use of library centers. *Reading Research Quarterly, 21*, 330–346.

Technology and Reading Comprehension *11*

Technology has the potential for facilitating reading comprehension instruction. It can provide motivating material for students to use. It can provide a change in the process of thinking about printed text. It can provide students with new ways of working independently from the teacher. And it can provide a medium for direct reading comprehension instruction.

The technology to be discussed in this chapter includes:

- microcomputers
- captioned television
- movies and film strips
- tape recorders
- video cameras
- overhead projectors

While this is not a complete listing of the technology available to teachers today, it does represent some of the major technology available to teachers for reading comprehension instruction. Technology seems to add interest to instruction that students might otherwise consider "more of the same thing." But it is much more than that. Technology can facilitate independent study. It can change the learning process for those who find the traditional techniques ineffective. It can relieve the teacher from some of the monitoring duties that can take so much time. And as stated before, it can be exciting.

At times the most difficult aspect of teaching is to gain student attention. Most students are fascinated with technology and find it easy to concentrate when lessons are presented by way of technology.

Of course, technology can do no better than the material provided for it by educators. At times this material has been excellent, and at other times it has been very poor. For example, the rush to provide software materials for microcomputers resulted initially in a very poor collection of programs for teachers to use. One could easily become disenchanted with the software and give up on the use of the technology. However, a good understanding of the value of the technology should encourage teachers to stay with it and use its potential to the maximum. We will present the values of the use of each technology and suggest its use to facilitate reading comprehension.

MICROCOMPUTERS

Computer technology has developed to the point that even beginning readers and writers can profit from its technology. While initially the micros were seen as neat ways to play games, it did not take long for educators to see their potential for education. This potential lies in three major areas:

- the facilitation of writing through word processing
- the fascination of independent study through software
- the use of programs to improve efficiency of direct instruction

While numerous students develop skills in computer languages, the three areas mentioned are of most impact. Developing computer language skills, while interesting to some, is a complex and time-consuming task. Most teachers will be most eager to profit from the word-processing capabilities of the micros and from the software that is being developed to individualize instruction.

Word Processing

There is ample evidence that the micro can facilitate the development of writing skills. Further evidence shows that writing skills facilitate reading comprehension skills.

Word processing programs make writing easy and fun. They make the chore of correcting one's mistake easy, so editing is not the chore it once was. In fact, students want to edit their writing and make the necessary corrections since it is so easy. There is no need for pencils and erasers and messy papers with a lot of errors. There is no need to rewrite entire papers because of a few errors. The micro lets students go back to their writing and correct, add, delete, and move things around in a few seconds. (We have done so several times while writing this section.) When writing becomes exciting instead of a chore, even beginning writers enjoy the activity.

Writing is a comprehension process. One must search for the meanings in one's mind to best express ideas for others. Then one must search for the best words to communicate those ideas. As one becomes more aware of the writing process, reading becomes easier. It was once thought that reading definitely had to be developed before writing, but it is quite clear today that early writers become good readers. The micro made the writing process easy and enjoyable, fast and efficient. With most of the word-processing programs available today the word-processing systems can be mastered in a few days.

With the use of a word processor and a printer, the students can see their final copy in very respectable format. That is, the final product looks professional. If the final product is not perfect, it can easily be corrected.

These advantages are not meant to undermine the need for good penmanship. Of course, we want students to develop penmanship skills to the highest level of their abilities. There will be many times

Dr. David Williams

in school when pencil-and-paper writing is necessary, and these skills should be developed. However, in today's world, every student should also develop word processing skills so as to be as flexible as possible with their writing alternatives.

Equipment needed includes:

- monitor
- microcomputer
- printer

It is also desirable to obtain a four- or six-outlet power strip so that all of the necessary electrical plugs can be used in one wall socket. It is best to get a power strip with a circuit breaker, which helps to reduce damage to the computer during an electrical storm.

Monitors usually come with white print on a black background or green print on a black background. One should examine and try each type of screen print and select the one with which one feels most comfortable. The color does not seem to matter much in terms of reading ease.

There are many micros on the market. In general, you get what you pay for. But there are sales and manufacturer's discounts, so it is best to shop around. Many dealers will make package deals with school systems for bulk purchases. However, if one is using money from PTA gifts or from special school funds, one becomes a shopper in a competitive marketplace. Since many people now own their own computers, it might be helpful to talk with some of them to get some tips on what a given micro can and cannot do.

There are many options on printers as well. Of course, the printer must be compatible with the micro. Dot-matrix printers are considerably cheaper than letter-quality printers. Originally, some dot-matrix printers were of very poor quality, now they, too, produce easily read text.

Software materials include:

- A word-processing program
- A supply of floppy discs
- A guide book for use with the word-processing program

Word-processing programs should be "user-friendly." That is, they should be understandable to the students without a lot of training. We suggest that the teacher try out the program before purchasing it. If the program is confusing to the teacher, it would probably be confusing to students. Some students are extremely computer literate and can handle complicated systems; however, many students will just be beginning to gain computer skills, so a user-friendly program is recommended.

Floppy discs are inexpensive. We recommend that each student have his or her own disc. That makes it possible for students to save and delete files as they like, without interfering with the files of others. Floppy discs are delicate, so students should be taught how to handle them and store them. A storage box should be obtained. Most computer stores have fancy disc file boxes, but the plain file box that we use serves the purpose very well.

Most programs have a book or booklet that explains all of the program functions and procedures for making those functions operative. If the teacher is not skilled in a given program, we suggest the purchase of a program book.

People who have computer skills are usually very willing to help beginners. We suggest that the teacher identify one or two such persons whom he or she can feel free to call upon for help. For example, when an operation is a bit technical, say, getting the program to print page numbers, instead of getting frustrated, we call our secretary and she gets us on track in a few seconds.

Revising and editing one's own writing is a demanding reading activity. Writers must read their own materials to be sure that the messages they are trying to communicate make sense, are presented in the best possible format, are accurate in spelling and grammar, and have used the very best vocabulary to communicate effectively. The revising and editing process provides one of the clearest examples of the connection between reading and writing. That connection should be explained to the students, and they should receive instruction and practice to enable them to appreciate that connection and to become skilled in switching from writing to reading and from reading to writing. Since many students have difficulty revising and editing their own work, the teacher will want to employ some instructional strategies to assist them. We have found teacher modeling and paired learning to be effective strategies.

As explained in Chapter 2, teachers can model by thinking aloud. After writing a few paragraphs, the teacher might say, "I think I'll read what I have written aloud to myself, to get a feeling of how it sounds." After reading a sentence or two, the teacher might stop and say, "That doesn't sound exactly right. Maybe I could use a stronger word to make that sentence more forceful." Or the teacher might say, "Maybe that second sentence should be the first sentence. I'll read it that way and see how it sounds." After revising the writing, the teacher can make the changes on the computer, print out a copy, and share the final product with the students. The students can then be encouraged to do the same and use reading as an aid to better writing. They will be likely to exclaim, "Hey, this works really well!"

Students can be paired for the revising and editing steps. Two students can read and react to each other's writing. This works very well for the editing step since many writers have difficulty seeing their own mistakes. For example, if a writer confused "there" for "their," he or she would not be likely to find the mistake by using the reading and thinking aloud strategy; the misused homophone would sound correct. Students will quickly learn that working in pairs results in an improved product. This activity places both students in a real-life critical reading situation.

Software

Computer software comes in a variety of packages whose quality varies just as the quality of printed materials varies. Almost all of these packages are copyrighted, so it is not legal to reproduce them. To avoid illegal reproduction, many of them are not available for review before purchase. There are clearinghouses, however, that provide reviews of software packages. Some distributers will permit a review of a portion of a software package to allow you to determine whether it is of the quality that would make it worth purchasing.

Computer software is designed to permit students to study independently. When well done, programs can be quite superior to the traditional materials available for independent study—workbooks, ditto sheets, and instructionally designed kits. There are several features that make programs superior to traditional materials:

1. Feedback. Most good programs provide the learners with immediate feedback about the accuracy of their responses. In most traditional materials feedback does not exist or is not immediate.
2. Personalized instruction. Many programs ask the students to type in their name at the beginning of the program. Then the feedback and other instructions can be personalized. For example, after Andrea has typed her name on the computer, the screen might show, "OK, Andrea, push any key to start." After doing some activities, the screen might show, "Good work, Andrea, you got all of these ten activities answered correctly—congratulations." Or it might show, "Andrea, you missed five of these ten activities.

Would you like to try again, Andrea? If so, push Return."
Students get a thrill out of seeing their name on the screen.

3. Branching. Some programs permit students to progress at
   different rates. For example, if there is a group of twenty
   activities and the student is successful on the first ten, the
   screen might show, "Andrea, you are doing very well. You
   do not need to continue with these activities. If you want
   to continue, push the Space Bar. If you want to go to the
   next set of activities, push Return." This type of programing
   allows for student decision making. If Andrea was having
   fun with her success and wants to continue, she can do so.
   However, if Andrea is bored and eager to move on, she can
   do that instead.

4. Simulation. Some programs use fancy graphics that allow
   for simulation activities. One well-known simulation program permits students to determine how much profit they
   can make by selling lemonade (Sell Lemonade, 1975). It
   includes arithmetic, reading, reasoning, and a bit of luck.
   The variables provided include the cost of the lemonade
   ingredients, weather conditions, the cost of signs, etc. Two
   or more students can participate, creating a simulation of
   actual lemonade stand competition. One nice feature is that
   students have fun while using their thinking skills.

There are many other features offered by high-quality software
programs; the ones presented above simply provide some basic examples of available features. When students have difficulty understanding the use of programs, the teacher can use those programs for
direct instruction. For example, direct instruction with *Lemonade
Stand* could involve discussion about why a lemonade stand might
do poorly on a rainy day or because of lack of advertising. After the
teacher thinks aloud about some of these variables and encourages
student discussion, this new information is used to make decisions
about how to run the lemonade stand. That information about the
decisions is entered into the simulation activity, and if the new information makes sense, the stand will make a better profit. It gives
a good comprehension lesson.

Of course, there are some limitations to the use of computers for instruction. Not all students can work with these programs at the same time. The teacher will need to establish management systems to provide equal access to the computer. Furthermore, while computers are sturdy instruments, they do break down. And software discs can easily be damaged.

We think that the advantages of computers far outweigh the disadvantages. But using computers is an individual decision for each teacher. There are other software programs that are designed for purposes other than reading comprehension, but which are highly motivating and have an impact on comprehension. There are several available which permit teachers or children to develop their own crossword puzzles. These programs provide a rich and different experience with word meanings. Other programs assist students to develop student newspapers—and the final product looks like a newspaper. Still others provide the ability to make banners and various kinds of award posters. These software programs add excitement and novelty to a reading comprehension program.

CAPTIONED TELEVISION

Since 1980 closed-captioned television has been available to hearing and hearing-impaired students as a medium for reading instruction. Little use has been made of it, however, because the educational community has not been informed of its potential. It is not uncommon to see an announcement on the television screen, "THIS SHOW IS CLOSED CAPTIONED FOR THE HEARING IMPAIRED." More than 160 hours of television are captioned every week, and those captions can be seen on any television set equipped with a decoder. The captions usually appear at the bottom of the television screen, enabling hearing-impaired viewers to read and understand what is being said on the program. Captions are not signs or fingerspellings; they are words.

It has been well documented that television has potential for teaching reading and thinking skills (Splaine, 1987; Kane, 1980; Mason & Mize, 1978). They list such reading comprehension skills as interpreting graphs and charts, making inferences, predicting outcomes,

HE'S ENJOYING
HIS NEW DIET.

HE'S ENJOYING HIS NEW DIET

recognizing persuasive language, separating fact from opinion, recognizing literary elements, and recognizing main ideas—that, and more, without captions. Now the potential is far greater with the availability of captioned television.

Open captions are commonly used during sporting events. They present information to the viewer about game statistics or other information that would be troublesome to repeat orally. While viewers can easily watch the show and gain information from the open captions, the public has resisted the idea of having open captions on popular television shows because it is felt that captions would be distracting. So the captions are closed and can be seen only if a decoder is attached to the television set. Who needs open captions on "Dynasty"? The hearing impaired need them. And captions might be useful to many hearing persons, too.

Recently there have been some research reports that indicate that many students could profit from viewing television with captions (Koskinen, Wilson, & Jensima, 1985; NCI, 1986). The captions seem to enhance reading sight vocabulary, reading comprehension, and oral reading fluency. Apparently, captioned television offers several advantages to some struggling readers:

1. It offers a highly motivating medium for reading instruction. Most students love to watch television. Their love for television can gain their attention during the process of learning to read.
2. It adds a multisensory element to the reading process. The drama of watching television, the sound of television, and the words appearing in the captions make captioned television a multisensory approach to the teaching of reading.
3. Most important, we believe, it changes the process for readers to comprehend. Comprehension comes first and the decoding of the words is secondary. Research tells us that students who have prior knowledge about a subject can read about it better than those who have none. For example, students who have visited the Space Museum in Washington, D.C., can have a better understanding of the development of air travel than those who have not had that experience. They read about the Lindbergh flight and recall having seen *The Spirit of St. Louis*; others can only imagine what that plane might have looked like, even if they have seen a picture of it. So it is with captioned television. The television supplies the meaning, and the captions help the students with the words.

Children are television literate by the age of six. That is, they can understand the shows appropriate for their age level without any adult interpretations. Other than primary experiences with an event or a topic, there is no other way for students to know, in advance, any information about the topic. For example, many of us have a lot of information about the United States' efforts in space technology. Most of us could come up with the names of astronauts, missions, or even the names of spacecrafts. That makes comprehension easier than if we asked ourselves for details of the Battle of Hastings. If an article were to be read about these two topics, most would agree that they would better comprehend the United States' efforts in space, not because the words are easier to read, but because they know more about the subject before they begin to read. Captioned television provides the background information that facilitates the ease of reading captions.

In order to use the technology of captioned television in the teaching of reading one needs the following equipment:

- a television set
- a caption decoder
- a video cassette recorder (VCR)

Any television set will do. It does not need to be a color television, although color adds to the impact of the program being viewed. Most schools have television sets for other instructional areas; these sets can be used for reading instruction as well.

Decoders can be obtained from a variety of sources. For example, the Sears catalogs list them. If a decoder cannot be located, call the National Captioning Institute in Falls Church, Va. (the phone number is 703–998–2400); they can get you in touch with the nearest retailer in your area. The decoder, which is attached to a television set much the same as a VCR, is lightweight, enabling almost anyone to make the installation. Decoders come with complete installation instructions.

A television set and a decoder will permit you to view captioned television live without a VCR. If, however, you want to view a show more than once for instructional purposes, the show will need to be recorded and shown again by means of a VCR. Many captioned shows and films can be obtained from your local video store. If you want to use these, you will need a VCR. We recommend a VHS-type VCR instead of the Beta system, since all shows are now being captioned on VHS. If you plan to obtain your video cassettes from your local video store, it would be wise to check with them concerning the type of cassettes they have available. If you plan to record live shows on your own equipment, you can use either VHS or Beta; it makes no difference. Remember that television programs are copyrighted materials: They can be used for educational purposes, but there are restrictions. Check with your media specialist to learn about those restrictions.

Since the only software needed will be the video cassettes, teachers should have no problems with software. We advise a careful review of the programs planned for use in schools for educational purposes. Obviously, some programs contain materials that would be inappropriate for use in the schools. We are not referring to the educational content of the shows; we are concerned with content that may not be appropriate to elementary school students. Many programs, however, are very suitable for educational purposes, for example, "3–2–1 Contact," "Sesame Street," and "Ripley's Believe It or Not."

Instruction with Captioned Television

Teachers can use the same instructional techniques with captioned television that they use for traditional print materials. They can develop meaningful sight vocabulary. They can provide instruction in all types of comprehension skills. They can develop oral reading fluency skills. To use captioned television for reading comprehension instruction, teachers will not need to learn new instructional techniques. The only thing that changes is the medium used for instruction. We have found that there are several features in television that facilitate some areas of reading comprehension in particular.

Vocabulary development. The use of figurative language is very common on television shows. Teachers can use those shows as an exciting way to present the notion of figurative language. In one show we found the following: "take in the sights," "pull your own weight," "breaking my heart," "teach those dogs a lesson," "hang in there," and "gives me the creeps." We asked the students to guess what these idioms mean. Then we let them view the program in an attempt to check their meanings in the program. When one appeared, we would push the Pause button for a discussion.

In another program we were able to introduce the following words after the students had watched the program: *orphan, strays, vicious,*

ballerina, *landlubbers*, and *dognappers*. The students not only pro-
nounced the words, but also had a thorough understanding of the
meaning of each word.

Prediction. Most television shows feature viewer prediction. If
the viewer is not actively predicting, the show quickly loses appeal.
We have had success showing very short segments of a show at a time
and then turning off the television so that the students can attempt
to predict what will happen next. The television is then turned on
again, and the students' predictions are determined to be accurate or
not accurate. (Note that, as mentioned earlier in this book, it does
not matter whether the predictions were accurate. In fact, many television shows attempt to lead the viewer to inaccurate predictions.
That develops the response, "Oh! I didn't think it would work out
that way." The lesson then helps the students go back and think about
what happened in the first part of the show to mislead them.)

For example, in one program of "Differ'nt Strokes" some of Arnold's relatives were visiting. The visiting relatives were dropping
water balloons on people passing by on the street below. We asked
the students, "What do you think Arnold will do?" They came up with
many logical predictions: "tell his father," "take the balloons away,"
"get out of there so he won't get blamed." None of those predictions
was correct, but the students were eager to find the answer. We had
them read the captions when the answer appeared in the program.

Problem solving. Television shows lend themselves to problem-
solving comprehension lessons very well. Most shows have many factors that go into the solutions of the show's problem. By helping
students identify those factors, they gain insight into the problem-
solving process. It is also possible to use the technique of changing
some of those factors to help students see how the problem might
have been solved differently under other circumstances. We have students look for the factors in the captions and jot them down so that
they can be discussed later after the problem has been solved in the
program.

Oral reading fluency. We have found that students can read
fluently from the scripts of shows that they have just watched. Of
course, fluent oral reading is an indication of good comprehension.
If a student reads a script from a short segment of "Sesame Street"

after viewing that segment, the oral reading is most likely to have the fluency of the actors in the show. Since scripts of shows are not usually available to teachers, copies of the captions must be made. We have used very short segments (one or two minutes) and have found it an easy task to make a copy of the captions. The effort has almost always been worth it because of the enthusiasm of the students when they get to read what they have just viewed. One girl in our reading clinic could not read fluently even when using her own language experience stories, but she loved reading the "Sesame Street" captions and did so fluently.

The technology has been developed for taking captions off the screen and onto a microcomputer. These captions can then be printed out. When that technology becomes available to teachers, the task of copying captions to make scripts will be eliminated.

The National Captioning Institute has developed a booklet for teachers on how to provide reading instruction via closed-captioned television (Koskinen, & Wilson, 1987). Lesson ideas and reading activities are included.

MOTION PICTURES AND FILM STRIPS

Most teachers will find it useful to use the technology of motion pictures and film strips for a variety of teaching activities. These media are useful in providing students with background knowledge they are unable to experience at first hand. For example, it is unlikely that many students, in a given class, have had firsthand experience with living in Africa or climbing tall mountains. Yet it would be useful for students to have some idea about these topics before they try to read about them and understand the meaning of the text. An easy and inexpensive way to give them background is the use of motion pictures or film strips.

Motion pictures and film strips come in two basic types of packages: those with captions and those without captions. For example, the National Geographic Society has developed film strips with and without captions on the same topics. As an aid to reading comprehension, we suggest that these media be used in the captioned format. The captions add the use of words as well as visual graphics to illustrate a concept or an experience. The captions are open; that is, no special equipment is needed to see them. Teachers might be well advised to consult their media specialist to know whether captions are available. If they are, we suggest that they be used if reading comprehension is a part of the objectives of the lesson. Teachers can also consult media catalogs to see whether captioned motion pictures and film strips are available. They are usually at or nearly at the same cost of noncaptioned materials. The advantage is rather obvious. The students not only gain knowledge of the topics being presented, but also see the words that these topics represent.

With or without captions, motion pictures and film strips provide a rich experience for many students. They bring unfamiliar concepts into lifelike view. When well done, they present accurate information that might not be presented to the students through any other medium. Most students cannot and should not be expected to understand the life of an Eskimo or the terror of a hurricane if they had not had that experience. But motion pictures and film strips can make up somewhat for the lack of firsthand experience. And, we'd add, they are even more effective with captions! Captions add the reading dimension to the visual drama. What better way for students to gain from the drama than also to experience the words that go with the drama?

The instructional activities to be used with captioned motion pictures and film strips are identical to those to be used with captioned television; that is, they are the same with any of the traditional instruction materials. The advantage is that they carry meaning in front of decoding, as does captioned television. This advantage seems to work very well with those students who have trouble with the traditional sequence of decoding first and then comprehending.

TAPE RECORDERS

Perhaps one of the most popular technologies, and the most accessible one, is the tape recorder. Tapes are sturdy and easy to store, making them less subject to destruction than the materials of some other technologies. Of course, through the careless handling of tapes, content that was to have been saved can be erased.

They can easily be used to facilitate reading comprehension. Students can use tape recorders to record their retelling of stories. They can then edit these retellings by adding to or deleting material from the contents on the tape. Even very young students can learn to operate the few controls, making this technology available to all students.

Students can use tape recorders to practice class presentations. Practice with a tape recorder provides students with audio feedback of their own voice, as well as feedback about the content of the planned presentation. Students can be taught to be constructively critical of themselves, a skill that can be directly applied to reading at a later time.

When the teacher wants students to practice fluent oral reading, the tape recorder is a valuable asset. Students can monitor their own oral reading. They can practice a given selection several times, making improvements with each additional reading. Fluent oral reading is one of the best indicators of how well students understand what they are reading. One positive aspect of the use of a tape recorder for oral reading practice is that it is private. If students make errors during the first reading, these errors can be corrected in subsequent readings without anyone being aware of them. Self-monitoring and self-correcting are skills needed by all students who seek to become independent learners.

At times, teachers will want their students to prepare a play relating to a story they have read. Each student takes the part of one of the characters from the story. Sometimes these plays are presented poorly because of a lack of adequate practice. Providing these students with a tape recorder for practice allows them to hear themselves and make changes to improve the quality of their play.

VIDEO CAMERAS

Video cameras have been used increasingly as a means of instruction in the elementary and middle schools. The cameras can record live actions of the students and preserve them on video cassettes, so they add video action to the audio action of the regular tape recorder.

The cameras are not difficult to use, and they can be attached to a tripod, eliminating the necessity for students to hold them. The tripod also permits taping free from the interference of motion. Once taped, the cassette can be played through a VCR on any television set. The cassettes can be edited by erasing or adding to sections, thus enabling students to create a fine final product. After viewing a portion of their video productions, students can self-critique or call upon some of their peers for a critique.

Students can produce short programs or entire shows, including school announcements and "commercials." When involved in these types of productions, students are required to use all of the thinking skills necessary for understanding written text.

They can produce programs about books they have read and experiences they have had in and out of school, and they can create their versions of some of their favorite television shows. They can document school events and portray events in history; they can preserve a science experiment or a school assembly. The use of the video camera as an aid to comprehension provides many creative opportunities for teachers to assist students to develop the skills needed for all types of comprehension.

OVERHEAD PROJECTORS

The overhead projector can easily be used by all students when they are interested in developing materials for class presentations. They require the use of transparencies upon which students can write, do art work, reproduce pictures, and develop charts and graphs for data presentations. Overhead projectors are available in almost all schools. Teachers will need to find and use the on–off switch and know how to change the projection bulb.

An advantage of the use of the overhead projector, over the use of a chalkboard or chart paper, is the ability of the person using the overhead projector to face the audience throughout the presentation. Overheads also allow for the presentation of visual information in greatly varying degrees of size. So for small groups the visual presentation can be small, and for large groups it can be screen size. This flexibility makes the overhead projector useful for all type of groups and everyone can see the visual information easily.

CHAPTER SUMMARY

In this chapter some of the technology that can aid instruction, and especially reading comprehension instruction, has been presented. With a little practice, teachers can learn to use this technology to enhance their lessons and create an interest in learning that may not otherwise be obtained. While there are many other types of technology available for teachers, these we have selected provide an overview of the potential that is currently available.

REFERENCES

Kane, H. (Ed.) (1980). *Critical Television Viewing*. New York: Cambridge Press.

Koskinen, P. & Wilson, R. (1987). *Have You Read Any Good TV Lately? A Guide for Using Captioned TV in the Teaching of Reading*. Falls Church, Va.: National Captioning Institute.

Koskinen, P., Wilson R., & Jensima, C. (1985). Closed-captioned television: A new technique for reading instruction. *Reading World*, 24:4, 1–7.

Sell Lemonade, (1975). Minnesota Educational Computing Consortium, St. Paul, Minnesota.

Mason, G., & Mize, J. (1978). Teaching reading with television. *Educational Technology*, 18:100, 5–11.

NCI. (1986). "Closed-captioned television: A new technology for enhancing reading skills for learning disabled students. Research Report 86–1. Falls Church, Va.: National Captioning Institute.

Splaine, J. (1987). *The Critical Viewing of Television*. South Hamilton, Mass.: Critical Thinking Press.

Assessment of Reading Comprehension

Most classroom teachers are interested in obtaining information about their students' reading comprehension abilities. Since there are several ways of obtaining such information, it is not always easy to decide which one to use. Teachers must first determine what questions they want to have answered by way of assessment activities. Those questions might include the following:

1. *Are my students placed in appropriate materials for instruction?* To answer that question teachers might choose to use teacher observation or teacher-made cloze or maze tests.
2. *Have my students mastered specific comprehension skills?* To answer that question teachers might choose teacher observation, teacher-made tests for specific objectives, or commercial criterion-referenced tests.
3. *How are my students comprehending, compared to other groups of students?* To answer that question teachers might choose standardized reading tests that have good comprehension subsections.
4. *Can my students answer questions about a text they have read? Do they respond well to various types of questions?*

To answer these questions teachers might choose to keep records of student responses to various types of questions over a period of time.

To answer each of these important questions, teachers will probably want to use more than one means of assessment. If the various means of assessment produce confirming results, teachers can feel comfortable with the answers. When they do not produce comfirming results, teachers must seek additional support information in order to answer their questions.

We present the four most common sources of assessment in reading comprehension in the elementary classroom and discuss their advantages and their limitations:

- teacher observation
- teacher-made tests
- criterion referenced tests
- standardized tests

We will not include some of the tests commonly used by reading specialists because this book has been prepared for classroom teachers. The four sources of information mentioned above are usually available for classroom teacher use.

Teachers will need to consider some of the following factors related to the sources of assessment information:

- expense
- time needed (individual versus group administration)
- ease of administration
- validity (does the test measure what it was designed to measure?)
- reliability (does the test measure accurately?)
- ease of interpretation

Problems with any of these factors might discourage a teacher from using a given assessment procedure.

The first two sources of assessment data (teacher observation and teacher-made tests) are curriculum based. Deno (1985) refers to these as curriculum-based measurement (CBM). CBM has several advantages over the traditional assessment procedure used in the schools. First, students are assessed with the materials used for instruction; that constitutes what is usually called "ecological validity." Second, by using the actual instruction materials in the assessment the teacher skips the difficult task of matching test scores with actual classroom practice. Third, in recent years there has been a growing support in the literature for the use of teacher evaluation of student progress— a form of evaluation that was suspect in the past. Recently research has shown that teacher judgments about student performance in the materials used for instruction is at least as valid as the tests produced by publishing companies (Nave, 1982). In fact, CBM can be used over time during the instructional year, providing multiple sources of data from which teachers can make appropriate decisions.

For instructional purposes CBM has major advantages over tests that require a match of test scores with the materials used in the curriculum. For example, one cannot assume that a student's standardized test score of 6.0 would mean that the student can read a sixth grade science text. On the other hand, a CBM assessment that a student can read a sixth grade science text is assuring because the student demonstrated reading skills in that text, not on a test unrelated to that text.

TEACHER OBSERVATION

Teachers make observations about student performance every day. For example, they might note that Pat is always the last one to finish silent reading activities, that Evan is a fluent oral reader, that Lynda has difficulty answering teacher questions about what has been read, that Elaine seems especially effective at making personal outlines. Such observations are ecologically valid since they are made during actual reading instruction. When observations are made over a period of time obtaining the same results, they can be considered reliable.

Informal notes taken about observations can help teachers keep a record of those behaviors. Such records are useful for student and parent conferences. They can also be useful when the teacher meets with school resource personnel about obtaining special services for students.

At times teachers might want to make observations in a more formal way. They might develop a checklist of some important behaviors so that they can simply use check marks to indicate that those behaviors have been observed. These checklists can be reproduced so that the teacher has one for each student. Student behaviors can be recorded so that the teacher has a sense of students' strengths and needs. Instruction can be adjusted for a period of time and then the checklist reused to determine improvement. For example, a teacher who wants to assess a group of students' abilities in answering questions that involve critical thinking can place these students in critical-thinking situations and evaluate their abilities as very good, good, fair, or poor. The teacher can then provide instruction in the use of critical-thinking skills. After several weeks of such instruction, the teacher can reevaluate the students' critical-thinking skills and compare their abilities with the preinstructional assessment.

While we strongly advocate the use of teacher observation as a reading comprehension assessment technique, we must add some words of caution. Teacher observations are subject to bias, that is, teachers might see what they want to see. Observations might be misinterpreted, resulting in inaccurate assessment. Teachers can do three things to overcome this difficulty.

First, they should try to make observations on student behaviors that are as inference-free as possible. Is what one is observing really what one thinks it is? For example, if one is trying to determine whether students are on- or off-task, one runs the risk of making assumptions about what is involved with on-task and off-task behavior. If a student is trying to answer a question and gazes out the window, a teacher might assume that to be off-task behavior; the student, however, might be deeply involved in thought about the appropriate answer. The assumption about off-task behavior is a misinterpretation of the student's behavior.

Second, teachers can try to obtain supportive data from other sources. They might try to confirm their observation with observations from another teacher or from test scores.

Third, they might want to determine whether this behavior is observed over time. A single occurrence of a given behavior is not suitable for an assessment conclusion. The main advantage of the use of teacher observation is that it can be obtained again and again. The repeated observation of a given behavior adds creditability to its being an accurate assessment of that behavior.

Even if we make these three checks on observation bias, bias might still be in operation. Part of observational bias has to do with thinking that you are seeing what you expected to see. For example, teachers might believe that poor readers cannot develop their own think-links. When poor readers are given an opportunity to do so, they might respond slowly, leading the teacher to believe they cannot develop their own think-links. Therefore, the teacher might be tempted to move in and provide direction, making the conclusion that poor readers cannot develop their own think-links. On the other hand, a teacher might be very certain that good readers can develop their own think-links. When given the opportunity to do so, they too might respond slowly, but in this case the teacher might think that they are just trying to be very careful. The teacher does not move in with help, but lets the good readers develop their own think- links, making the conclusion that good readers can develop their own think-links. Observational biases lead the teacher to different interpretations and different teacher reactions.

However, this is not a reason to be discouraged, so long as teachers try their utmost to make careful observations, record those observations, and are always alert to the possibility of observer bias.

TEACHER-MADE TESTS

All teachers rely upon teacher-made tests for assessment in all areas of instruction. They usually involve CBM, because teachers are interested in whether students have been able to learn from the instruction provided, that is, the curriculum. Teacher-made tests are usually directed to very specific learnings. For example, after a health unit on the care of teeth, a teacher might construct a test to determine what students have learned about dental health. Such tests are usually short quizzes that can be administered rather quickly.

The value of teacher-made tests for assessment of reading comprehension is directly related to the care taken in their construction. If the teacher asks questions that call for various types of thinking, he or she can obtain much valuable assessment information. On the other hand, if the teacher asks only those easily developed literal questions, the assessment information received is seriously limited. Likewise, if the teacher-made tests are extremely short, the tests will likely suffer from a lack of reliability. Longer tests allow students to miss several items and still demonstrate knowledge of what that test is measuring.

When teachers decide to use teacher-made tests to assess reading comprehension, they have a major decision to make: Should they make subjective tests or objective tests? Subjective tests are easy to construct but difficult to evaluate; objective tests are much more difficult to construct but easier to evaluate. For example, teachers might develop a very subjective and open-ended test about a passage that has been read: "Write all that you can remember about what Roberta did in this story." That type of test would be easy to develop, but it might be very difficult to evaluate the students' responses in a fair and accurate manner. On the other hand, teachers might develop a fifteen-item test on important events in the passage just read. While such a test might take some time to develop, it would be much easier to evaluate. If Gwen was able to answer all fifteen items accurately and Spencer could only answer five of the fifteen items, the teacher would have a relatively good assessment of those two students' comprehension of that passage.

Unfortunately, the decision about which type of test to develop and use is not that simple. Subjective tests allow students to sort through ideas in the passage and to decide which of those ideas they think they should include in their answers. On the other hand, objective tests limit the student to respond to just those items included. They might have had a lot of important information from the passage that was not included in the test questions. The result is that teachers, in these cases, obtain incorrect information about what some students were really able to comprehend.

We recommend that teachers use both types of assessment. By moving from objective to subjective tests and back again, teachers can make assessments, over time, that help them to understand the nature of their students' reading comprehension abilities. We view the exclusive use of one type of assessment as a serious mistake.

As with teacher observation, record keeping is extremely important when using teacher-made tests. The advantage of both of these CBM assessment techniques is that they can be used over time, resulting in a pattern of performance not derivable from a one-time assessment. If, however, teachers do not keep records of performances, the advantage of over-time assessment is lost, for there will be no patterns of student performance to observe.

At times teachers will need to determine students' abilities to read from various texts. There are two ways that teachers can do this. One is for the teacher to ask students to read a couple of sample paragraphs aloud in a private session. For the best assessment of comprehension, we suggest that the students read the paragraph silently before the oral reading session with the teacher. Teachers can assess oral reading fluency and accuracy in such informal settings. Fluent reading usually means that the students understand the text and can read it with expression. Accurate reading of the words usually means that the words are in the students' sight vocabularies. When the students can read with fluency and accuracy, the teacher can assume that the text is appropriate for them.

When teachers sample students' oral reading, they will need to find the time for one-on-one testing. Students should not be assessed in front of their peers. When students are experiencing a difficult time with the text, the teacher can excuse them from reading any more or the teacher can change the text to something easier without embarrassment to the student.

Teachers can also develop informal *cloze* tests to help them determine the appropriateness of a given text for a group of students. Teachers can take several passages of about a hundred words each. Leaving the first sentence intact, they can delete every fifth word, leaving a blank space in which the students can write a word that they think fits. The cloze test might look something like this: "Mary had a little lamb. It's fleece was white _____ snow. Everywhere that Mary _____ the lamb was sure _____ go." For a given sample, twenty blank spaces should give the teacher a good indication of text appropriateness. By sampling several sections of the text, teachers can avoid the possible problem that one sample might be unrepresentative of the text, that is, too difficult or too easy. When students can complete 40 percent or more of the blanks accurately, teachers can assume that they can read and comprehend the text. We have a few suggestions about cloze test construction:

1. Do not delete proper nouns. Students often have no clues about the appropriate proper noun.
2. Do not delete the first word in a sentence. The first word is often key to understanding the sentence.
3. Leave the first and last sentences intact. This permits a good beginning and a good ending experience.
4. Make all the blanks the same length. The clues to the correct word should be from the words around it, not the length of the blank.

One problem with cloze tests is that they can be very frustrating to students who cannot comprehend the text. While administering a cloze test, the teacher should watch for signs of student frustration and excuse those students from completing the test. The advantage of cloze testing is that it can be done with groups of students. Since their responses are in writing, their privacy is protected.

An alternative to informal, teacher-made close texts is *maze* testing (Guthrie, 1974). Maze tests are similar to cloze tests with two important differences:

1. Instead of leaving a blank for every fifth word, choices are provided by the teacher. One choice is actually the word deleted, another is a word that is the same part of speech as the one deleted, and the last is a word that is a different part of speech from the one deleted. The maze test might look something like this:

Mary had a little lamb. Its fleece was white <u>the   </u> <u>little   </u> snow.
<u>as   </u>

Everywhere that Mary <u>went   </u>
<u>spend   </u>
<u>dog   </u>

the lamb was sure <u>swim   </u>
<u>to   </u> go."
<u>for   </u>

In maze tests students simply circle the word that makes the most sense.

2. The second difference is that a 70 percent correct score is needed with cloze tests, instead of the 40 percent correct score needed with maze tests.

We have found that maze tests are more difficult to develop than cloze tests, but they are easier to score and seem to be less frustrating for the students who take them. Both maze and cloze tests provide useful information about the appropriateness of text assignments.

CRITERION REFERENCED TESTS

Criterion referenced rests (CRT) might or might not be CBM. If they are developed and used with the materials used for instruction, they can be considered CBM. However, if they are developed by persons unfamiliar with the curriculum, they are not considered CBM. For example, a publishing company might develop a CRT based upon their research of useful objectives for reading comprehension in fourth grade classrooms. Since the CRT is not developed using the materials used in every fourth grade classroom, it cannot be considered CBM, even though they might be a very good CRT.

CRTs have been designed by most publishers of commercial materials to aid teachers in the assessment of student progress in those materials. Test items are developed for the various objectives of the materials used for instruction. Teachers are directed to use a CRT before instruction, provide the needed instruction, and then use the CRT again. The pretest–posttest usage is designed to let teachers know about student gains as a result of instruction. The idea of the use of CRT is a good one. The notion that CRT assesses student progress based on instructional objectives can be of help to teachers. Whether these texts actually measure student progress is open to some question. Some CRTs use too few items to assess an objective; for example, if the objective is to understand the main idea and the test includes only two test items, test reliability is questionable. Moreover, if the test items are not related to the teacher's instruction, the test is not a valid CRT for that teacher's students.

If these problems can be overcome, the use of CRTs add a very valuable component to CBM. If they cannot be overcome, CRT usefulness is greatly limited. While many publishing companies make great claims about the value of these CRTs, we urge teachers to use them with caution. As mentioned above, when they fit the curriculum and have enough items to warrant reliability, they can be used as one of the comprehensive assessment measures.

Many states now require the passing of CRTs for graduation from high school or for in-school promotion from grade to grade. These states are reacting to pressure from their constituents for educational accountability, but one must wonder about the effects such requirements have on the curriculum. Should a test or should educators determine the curriculum? It is clear to us that the latter is the correct choice, but that choice has limited value if the decisions made are based on political decisions as a result of public pressure. When states use passing CRTs as a condition for promotion or for graduation, they are seriously interfering with educators' professional responsibility for the development of curriculum, because when that happens teachers develop a curriculum to teach to the test whether or not they agree with the test objectives.

STANDARDIZED TESTS

Most teachers will have standardized test scores available to them, since most schools require their use. Standardized test scores on reading comprehension measures are of limited use as assessments of an individual student's reading comprehension. Of course, very high or very low scores do indicate the ease or the difficulty of the test and can be interpreted to indicate good and poor readers. But there are some serious problems:

1. If the scores are reported in grade equivalents, they cannot be interpreted to be reading grade levels. A fifth grader who obtains a grade equivalent of 7.5 may or may not be able to read a text for seventh grade level. Likewise, a fifth grader who obtains a score of 3.0 may or may not be able to read a text for third grade level. Grade equivalent scores are statistically determined and are not meant to be interpreted as reading levels.

2. If the scores are reported as percentiles, the teacher has some idea about how a given student compares with his or her peers. A percentile score of 75 indicates that 74 percent of this student's peers scored lower and 24 percent of this student's peers scored higher than he or she. While that may be interesting, it is difficult to interpret for any instructional adjustments that might be appropriate for these students.

3. Group standardized test results provide teachers and school officials with information about how groups of students have performed. Interpreting an individual student's score on a group standardized test as an indication of that student's reading comprehension performance is a *misuse* of that test score. On a given day a student might perform poorly for many reasons: fatigue, not feeling well, personal problems, room temperature, or just having a bad day in general, to mention a few. On another day, that same student might perform very well when such factors have improved. While these conditions might be in operation in any testing situation, they are a larger problem in the *one-time* testing situation used by group standardized tests.

4. The ability of students to respond to the topic of the test items creates another problem. Students who have never lived in a large city might have difficulty with test passages

about life in New York City, but they might do very well on passages about life on a farm. Students who have English as a second language might have difficulty relating to passages that reflect common knowledge about the way of life in America, but they are likely to have much useful information about ways of life in other cultures. Most test constructors make careful attempts to avoid the use of topics that are culturally biased. Unfortunately, that is an effort that is difficult to achieve. The problem is that some students might appear unable to respond to a main idea, read critically, or interpret items when in fact they do have the skills required but have no idea about the meaning of a passage whose topic is completely unfamiliar to them: The teacher might mistake such students as being unskilled in an area of reading comprehension.

5. Group standardized tests are only useful in a general way in the assessment of reading comprehension. It is usually difficult to be certain about what a reading comprehension score really means.

While standardized test scores are readily available to most teachers, they should be used with caution: Their use for making instructional decisions is extremely limited.

CHAPTER SUMMARY

Four of the common sources for comprehension assessment that are available to teachers have been discussed. The advantages and limitations of each source have also been discussed. A case was made for CBM, along with examples of this type of assessment. We hope that teachers will use the ideas in this book. They should decide about what is useful, making adjustments for the population that they are teaching. Remember, you are the *decision maker* in most of your teaching situations.

REFERENCES

Deno, S. (1985). Curriculum-based measurement: The emerging alternative. *Exceptional Children*, 52:3, 219–232.

Guthrie, J. T. (1974). The maze techniques to assess, monitor reading comprehension. *The Reading Teacher*, 28:2, 161–168.

Nave, D. (1982). Teacher judgment as a primary measure of reading performance. Unpublished doctoral dissertation, University of Maryland.

INDEX